A Catalogue Of The Shells Contained In The Collection Of The Late Earl Of Tankerville: Arranged According To The Lamarckian Conchological System

George Brettingham Sowerby

A

CATALOGUE

OF THE

SHELLS

CONTAINED IN THE COLLECTION

OF THE LATE

EARL OF TANKERVILLE,

ARRANGED ACCORDING TO THE

Lamarckian Conchological System;

TOGETHER WITH

AN APPENDIX,

CONTAINING

DESCRIPTIONS OF MANY NEW SPECIES,

BY

G. B. SOWERBY, F. L. S. &c.

ILLUSTRATED WITH SEVERAL COLOURED PLATES.

(9)

London:

Printed by E. J. Stirling, 20, Ironmonger Lane, Cheapside,

FOR G. B. SOWERBY, 156, REGENT STREET.

1825.

INTRODUCTORY
OBSERVATIONS.

On the occasion of opening for public inspection the matchless and celebrated Collection of Shells formed with such exquisite judgment and taste by the late Earl of Tankerville, and now confided to me by his Lordship's executors, for sale, some explanation of the particular object in view, and of the manner in which we intend to proceed, may appear to be necessary.

This Collection having been left by his Lordship to his executors for sale, it became a subject of regret to many who in common with ourselves are well-wishers to science, (and who see a greater probability of its being made scientifically useful by its being preserved entire than if sold in detail) that so noble a collection should be ultimately dispersed. Several plans have therefore been devised for preserving at least the important part of the Collection entire, none of which have, however, as yet been fortunate in their issue. I have therefore determined, having first made a Catalogue, to open the Collection for public inspection, in order that a just estimate may be formed of its real merits; in the mean time the duplicates are offered to the Public at prices fixed in a copy of the Catalogue to be kept in the room; and after two months shall have elapsed from the time of the first opening, the Shells forming the principal Collection will be also offered to the Public, unless an eligible offer should previously be made for them by private contract; and it is hoped that the opportunity thus afforded to any public institution to enrich their museum by the addition of so valuable a collection will not be neglected.

This Catalogue is necessarily incomplete, because the actual state of our knowledge in Conchology would not permit us to make it such as we could have wished it to be to meet the public eye. It will be observed, that this Collection consists of nearly 2500 species, many of which are only known by imperfect descriptions, and many others, if they be described at all, are with difficulty recognizable by the published descriptions, so that in many instances we have been compelled to leave blanks, to be filled up as future acquirements in this branch of science will permit, at the end of each genus. In order to make this little work more interesting than a mere Catalogue would be, we have ventured to add in an Appendix a short description of some of those Shells which we have good reason to believe have not been previously published by any author. We have also added a few coloured plates, in general representing some of the Shells we have so described, and in one or two instances these plates are of well known but extremely rare species. Among the latter is the Conus Gloria-Maris, of which shell we have never

seen more than two specimens, namely, that which
is in Mr. Saulier's Collection in Paris, and that which
adorns the present Collection. The faithful representation we have given of it will prove to all who
have seen the specimen in Mr. Saulier's Collection,
that ours is by far the finer, both in respect of size
and colour.

In making the Catalogue we have frequently been
puzzled by the discrepancies between Lamarck's descriptions and the figures to which he has referred,
and sometimes by his referring to figures of two very
different shells for the same species; we have, however, endeavoured to ascertain, by a comparison of
his description with the figures cited, which of the
shells he meant: in some cases this has enabled us
to decide; in others, where we could not decide, we
have expressed our doubt. It will be obvious to
every conchological student that Lamarck's work is
very incomplete, and that many species that have
been long well known are not to be found there; to
these we have given the specific names which we
have ascertained in other authors, joining them to
their proper Lamarckian Genera. Some of the obvious modern improvements have also been adopted,
particularly several new genera, of which the characters have been published since the appearance of
Lamarck's *Hist. Nat. des Anim. sans Vert.* In a few
instances, also, we have ventured to change the
places of some of the species from genera in which
they have been placed by mistake, to others with
which they accord perfectly.

In order to prevent as far as possible any misconception of the plan upon which we mean to proceed in the sale of this splendid Collection, we request that it may be particularly observed, that for the first two months from the opening of the Collection for public inspection, *the duplicates alone can be disposed of*, and that they may be paid for and taken away as soon as the purchasers please; the principal Collection, however, that is, the best specimen of every species, together with the varieties, are retained for the whole of the season; and in order to allow time for arranging any offer that may be made for the whole, they cannot be in any manner disposed of until after the 1st of April, or two months after the opening. It is also requested to be clearly understood that no pledge can be given for the disposal of any specimen from the principal Collection until that time, when those who are desirous of securing any specimen or part of the Collection will take care to bring or send their lists, ready marked, together with the amount according to the priced Catalogue. This plan of proceeding, which is the only one we can devise for securing to ourselves the means of disposing of the entire Collection, and for giving to every one a fair opportunity of inspecting it, and making their selection, is obviously open to one inconvenience; viz. that of several persons desiring to secure the same article: in such cases the preference must be given to that person who has first expressed his desire and performed the conditions: but if the right of priority cannot be decided, that person shall have the preference who shall ultimately offer the higher advanced price.

In conclusion, we have first to acknowledge our obligation to W. Swainson, Esq. for his descriptions of four new species of the Genus Mitra; in the knowledge of which, having made it his particular study, every Conchologist will readily acknowledge his pre-eminence: secondly, to state that this Catalogue has been written under such numerous disadvantages, that we have reason to fear some important errors may have crept in, for which we trust every allowance will be made by the candid scientific reader.

156, *Regent Street,*

CATALOGUE

OF THE

SHELLS

IN THE COLLECTION

OF THE LATE

EARL OF TANKERVILLE.

~~~~~~~~~~~~~~~

SILIQUARIA.

1 Siliquaria anguina,—*(a)* A large specimen, perfect at both terminations: *(b)* a small rose-
coloured specimen
2 ————— muricata

DENTALIUM.

3 Dentalium elephantinum
4 ————— aprinum
5 ————— octogonum
6 ————— Dentalis
7 ————— Entalis

SPIRORBIS.

8 Spirorbis nautiloides

A

SERPULA.

9 Serpula vermicularis
10 ———— fascicularis
11 ———— Intestinum
12 ———— contortuplicata
13 ———— glomerata
14 ———— decussata
15 ———— Infundibulum,—*(a)* with an Ostrea, upon Avicula spinosa, Nob.—*(b)* upon a large Serpula
16 ———— filograna
17 ———— Vermicella
18 ———— echinata, — *(a)* with its operculum, grouped upon Chamæ, &c.; two small specimens on Lace Coral
19 ———— sulcata
20 ———— dentifera, *(a)* var. upon a piece of Coral; and with its opercula
21 ———— lumbricalis, Dillw. *(a)* a large group attached to a Chama; *(b)* detached specimens
22 ———— *fuscata*
23 ———— *maxima*
24 ———— *tricuspidata*

VERMILIA.

25 Vermilia triquetra, on Buccinum undatum, and on Pecten obsoletus; *(a)* ead. var. testâ rubrâ, on Ostrea Crista-galli

GALEOLARIA.

26 Galeorlaria decumbens, *Sowerby;* *(a)* on Emarginula aspera; *(b)* on a Buccinum

MAGILUS.

27 Magilus antiquus

TUBICINELLA.

28 Tubicinella Balænarum; *(a)* a large specimen of Whale skin, containing many Tubicinellæ; *(b)* a separate specimen

CORONULA.

29. Coronula Diadema, two specimens; *(a)* a small and very perfect specimen upon a piece of Whale's skin

30 ———— balænaris, several specimens; *(a)* a piece of Whale's skin containing two.

31 ———— testudinaria

BALANUS.

32 Balanus sulcatus; *(a. b.)* adhering to Modiola albicostata? *(c)* var. of a lilac colour, with interrupted ribs; *(d)* upon Pecten varius

33 ———— Tintinnabulum, *(a)* conical with a broad base; *(b)* conical, ventricose; *(c)* elongated, scarcely ventricose

34 ———— calycularis; *(a. b)* adhering to Buccina

35 ———— ovularis; *(a)* upon the Strobilus of a Fir

36 ———— perforatus, *(a)* on a Patella; *(b)* on a Haliotis

37 ———— spinosus; *(a)* with the opercula detached; *(b)* attached to another] Balanus; *(c)* adhering to a fragment of a Balanus

38 ———— radiatus

39 ———— punctatus

40 ———— balanoides. Lepas balanoides, Dillw.

41 ———— crispatus? of a dark violaceous colour

42

43

44

45

46 Balanus
47

CONIA, Leach.

48 Conia Lyonsii, Leach
49 ——
50 —— porosa, *Sowerby*
51 —— purpurascens, Leach

ACASTA.

52 Acasta Glans, several individuals from a compact sponge, Ceylon

ANATIFERA.*

53 Anatifera lævis; *(a)* on a reed
54 —— striata

POLLICIPES.

55 Pollicipes Cornucopiæ, two fine groups

ASPERGILLUM.

56 Aspergillum Javanum
57 —— vaginiferum, a magnificent specimen
58 —— *sparsum*

FISTULANA.

59 Fistulana gregata, several groups and single specimens

SEPTARIA.

60 Septaria arenaria, one large tube

---

* Anatifa, Lam.

PHOLAS.

61 Pholas Dactylus
62 —— orientalis
63 —— crispata
64 —— costata
65 —— clavata

SOLEN.

66 Solen Vagina
67 —— truncatus, Dillw.—(a) var. somewhat tapering towards its rounded end
68 —— Siliqua
69 —— Ensis
70 —— ambiguus
71 —— Cultellus
72 —— planus
73 —— Legumen
74 —— Dombeyi
75 —— constrictus?
76 —— strigilatus
77 —— radiatus
78 —— violaceus
79 —— rostratus
80 —— Gigas, *Wood*
81 —— minimus, Gmel. probably the young shell of S. Gigas
82 —— Gigas? var. anticè subattenuata
83 —— truncatus, var. colore roseo marmorata

PANOPÆA.

84 Panopæa Aldrovandi

GLYCYMERIS.

85 Glycymeris Siliqua

MYA.

86 Mya truncata
87 —— arenaria

ANATINA.

88 Anatina truncata
89 ———— subrostrata
90 ———— globulosa
91 ———— trapezoïdes
92 ———— myalis

LUTRARIA.

93 Lutraria Solenoïdes
94 ——— elliptica
95 ——— rugosa
96 ——— tellinoïdes? Tellina angulata, Linn.;
    Chemn. vi. t. 9. f. 74. 75
97 ——— papyracea.—*Obs.* This Shell accords
    with Lamarck's description, but not with
    either of the figures he cites

MACTRA.

98 Mactra gigantea, one large, and two small
    specimens
99 ——— Spengleri
100 ——— striatella
101 ——— carinata
102 ——— helvacea
103 ——— grandis
104 ——— Stultorum, and varieties
105 ——— Australis
106 ——— violacea
107 ——— turgida
108 ——— plicataria
109 ——— rufescens

110 Mactra maculata
111 ———— subplicata
112 ———— alba
113 ———— solida
114 ———— Brasiliana
115 ———— depressa
116 ———— *elegans*
117 ———— *aspersa*
117* ———— solidissima? *Say*

CRASSATELLA.

118 Crassatella Kingicola
119 ———————— sulcata
120 ———————— rostrata
121 ———————— *radiata*

ERYCINA, Sowerby.

122 Erycina striata
123 ————
124a ———— complanata
125 ————
126 ———— æquilatera, *Gray*
127 ———— plebeia; Donax plebeia, *Mont.*

SOLENIMYA.

128 Solenimya Mediterranea

AMPHIDESMA.

129 Amphidesma cordiforme, Nob.; Tellania cordi-
    formis, Chemn. xi. t. 199, f. 1941. 1942
130 ———— reticulatum.   Tellania reticulata,
    Dillw.

PANDORA.

131 Pandora flexuosa, *Sowerbys' Genera of Shells*

SAXICAVA.

132 Saxicava rugosa
133 ————
134

PETRICOLA.

135 Petricola lamellosa?
136 ———— monstrosa, Nob.; Venus monstrosa, Dillw.
137 ———— pholadiformis

VENERIRUPIS.

138 Venerirupis perforans
139 ———— exotica?

LITHODOMUS.

140 Lithodomus Dactylus, Sowerby
141 ———— caudigerus, Id.

SANGUINOLARIA.

142 Sanguinolaria occidens
143 ———— rosea
144 ———— livida
145 ———— rugosa

PSAMMOBIA.

146 Psammobia virgata
147 ———— maculosa
148 ———— cærulescens
149 ———— Tellinella

PSAMMOTÆA.

150 Psammotæa *carnea*

TELLINA.

151 Tellina radiata
152 ———— unimaculata
153 ———— semizonalis?
154 ———— maculosa
155 ———— virgata, numerous varieties
156 ———— Spengleri
157 ———— rostrata
158 ———— latirostrata *(a)* var. pallida
159 ———— sulphurea
160 ———— foliacea
161 ———— operculata
162 ———— punicea
163 ———— depressa
164 ———— pulchella
165 ———— Fabula
166 ———— tenuis
167 ———— exilis
168 ———— donacina
169 ———— Remies
170 ———— sulcata
171 ———— striatula
172 ———— scobinata
173 ———— crassa
174 ———— lævigata; *(a)* radiis aurantiis nullis
175 ———— Lingua-felis
176 ———— rugosa
177 ———— lacunosa.—*Obs.* This shell is not properly placed among the Tellinæ; it rather belongs to Lamarck's Sanguinolariæ, or Psammobiæ
178 ———— Gargadia
179 ———— Brasiliana

180 Tellina bimaculata, many varieties
181 ———— Pristis
182 ———— sexradiata; which is only a variety of
    bimaculata .
183 ———— ostracea
183a———— carnaria *auctorum;* restored to this place,
    because it accords better with Tellina than
    with Lucina, to which Lamarck has removed it
184 ———— *pulcherrima*
185 ————
186 ————
187 ————
188 ————
189 ————
190 ————
191 ————
192 ————
193 ————
194 ————
195 ————
196 ————

TELLINIDES.

197 Tellinides Timorensis
198 ———— *ovalis,* (Tellina ovalis, Budgin M.S.)
199 ———— *emarginatus*
200 ———— *truncatulus*
201 ———— *politus*

CORBIS.

202 Corbis fimbriata

LUCINA.

203 Lucina Jamaicensis
204 ———— Pensylvanica

205. Lucina edentula ; *(a)* var. albida, gibbosior
206 ——— Childrenæ, Gray, in Annals of Philosophy
(1824) *(a. b.)* 2 specimens: one being the
reverse of the other
207 ——— Tigerina, Cytherea tigerina, *Lam.*
207*a* ——— ——— var. 3, subgronosa, *Lam.*
208 ——— punctata. Cytherea punctata, *Lam.*—
Obs. The two last species are removed from
the place which Lamarck assigned to them
among his Cythereæ, on account of their strict
accordance with the generic character of
Lucina
209 ——— divaricata
210 ——— squamosa
211 ——— globularis

DONAX.

212 Donax Scortum
213 ——— pubescens
214 ——— cuneata, numerous specimens and varieties
215 ——— compressa
216 ——— deltoides ; *lævigata, Dillw.* numerous varieties in colour
217 ——— radians
218 ——— ringens
219 ——— rugosa
220 ——— elongata
221 ——— denticulata
222 ——— Meroe
223 ——— scripta
223*a* ——— ——— var. tumidior
223*b* ——— ——— var. compressa, suborbicularis
224 ——— Trunculus
225 ——— Fabagella
226 ——— transversa

227 Donax incarnata, Chemn. vi. p. 265, tab. 26, f. 259
228 ———— æquilatera. An Venus donacina, Chemn. xi. p. 231, t. 202, f. 1985 & 1986?

CAPSA.

229 Capsa lævigata
230 ———— Brasiliensis

CRASSINA; Astarte, SOWERBY.

231 Crassina sulcata. Venus sulcata, Montagu.

CYRENA.

232 Cyrena fuscata
233 ———— fluminea
234 ———— violacea
235 ———— Caroliniensis? cyprinoides, Gray
236 ———— Bengalensis?
236a———— Sumatrensis, Sowerby
237 ———— Zeylanica

GALATHEA (Magadesma, BOWDICH.)

238 Galathea radiata

CYPRINA.

239 Cyprina Islandica

CYTHEREA.

240 Cytherea lusoria
241 ———— petechialis, several varieties
242 ———— impudica, several varieties
243 ———— castanea
244 ———— zonaria, many varieties
245 ———— graphica?

246 Cytherea morphina ? several
247 ———— purpurata ?
248 ———— casta
249 ———— Corbicula
250 ———— tripla
251 ———— gigantea
252 ———— Erycina
252a———— ———— var. 2, Lam. an potius species distincta?
253 ———— lilacina
254 ———— Chione, numerous varieties, and many stages of growth
255 ———— maculata, numerous varieties, and many stages of growth
256 ———— læta, several varieties
257 ———— impar
258 ———— castrensis, several varieties
259 ———— ornata
260 ———— ornata var?
261 ———— picta
262 ———— tigrina
263 ———— sulcatina ?
264 ———— juvenilis
265 ———— rufa ?
266 ———— guineensis
267 ———— Dione
268 ———— Arabica
269 ———— exoleta
270 ———— lincta var.
271 ———— concentrica
272 ———— prostrata
274 ———— scripta
275 ———— muscaria
276 ———— pulicaris
277 ———— pectinata
278 ———— gibbia
279 ———— divaricata

280 Cytherea rugifera
281 ———— flexuosa
282 ———— testudinalis
283 ———— citrina?
284 ———— aurantia.   The large Orange Venus,
from the South Seas; two large and one young
specimens
285 ————
286 ————
287 ————
288 ————
289 ————
290 ————
291 ————
292 ————
293 ————
294 ————
295 ————
296 ————
297 ————
298 ————
299 ————
300 ————
301 ————
302 ————
303 ————
304 ————
305 ————

VENUS.

306 Venus Puerpera var.
307 ———— ———— var.
308 ———— reticulata
309 ———— Corbis
310 ———— crenulata
311 ———— verrucosa

312 Venus rugosa
313 ——— Casina
314 ——— crebrisulcata
315 ——— plicata
316 ——— cancellata, numerous varieties.
316a——— ——— var: 2 Lam.
317 ——— granulata
318 ——— Marica
319 ——— cardioides
320 ——— mercenaria
321 ——— Lagopus
322 ——— Gallina
323 ——— lamellata
324 ——— exalbida
325 ——— Malabarica
326 ——— ——— var. testâ posticè plicatura
    flexuosâ
327 ——— papilionacea
328 ——— adspersa
329 ——— punctifera
330 ——— turgida
331 ——— litterata, three varieties and many spe-
    cimens
332 ——— sulcaria
333 ——— Textile
334 ——— texturata
335 ——— decussata, many varieties
336 ——— pullastra; (a) testâ monstrosâ
337 ——— aurea var.
338 ——— virginea
339 ——— scalarina?
340 ——— opima, several varieties in colour
340a——— nebulosa. An testâ junior speciei præ-
    cedentis
341 ——— laterisulcata?
342 ——— florida, several varieties
343 ——— Paphia, Dillw.

344 Venus fasciata, Id.
345 ———— fiammea, Lam.
346 ———— chinensis, Dillw.; obesa, Solander
347 ———— Tiara, Dillw.
848 ———— ———— ætate ventricosius?
349 ———— lamellosa, Chemn. vɪ. p. 298, t. 28, f. 293
        and 294
350 ————
351 ————
352 ————
353 ————
354 ————

VENERICARDIA.

354a Venericardia australis? one very large specimen
354b ———————— *crassicostata*

CARDIUM.

355 Cardium costatum
356 ———— ringens
357 ———— Asiaticum
358 ———— tenuicostatum
359 ———— fimbriatum
360 ———— bullatum
361 ———— papyraceum
362 ———— pseudo-lima
363 ———— aculeatum
364 ———— erinaceum, four full grown and two
        young specimens
365 ———— ciliare
366 ———— tuberculatum, many of the varieties
        of this shell are Card. rusticum of Wood
367 ———— lsocardia
368 ———— muricatum
369 ———— marmoreum
370 ———— elongatum

371 Cardium ventricosum
372 ———— rugosum
373 ———— sulcatum
374 ———— serratum
375 ———— lævigatum
376 ———— biradiatum
377 ———— Æolicum
378 ———— rusticum, *Chemn.* vɪ. t. 19, f. 197
379 ———— Grœnlandicum
380 ———— Islandicum, Chemn. vɪ. t. 19, f. 195
& 196, two very large and one small specimen, probably Card. crenulatum, *Lam.*
381 ———— latum, two varieties
382 ———— Unedo
383 ———— medium
384 ———— Fragum
385 ———— retusum
386 ———— hemicardium
387 ———— Cardissa
388 ———————— var. valvarum carinâ muticâ
389 ———— inversum
390 ———— Junonium
391 ———— angulatum?
392 ———— papyraceum
393 ————
394 ————

CARDITA.

395 Cardita sulcatus
396 ———— ajar, several varieties in colour; *(a)* a
distorted specimen
397 ———— turgidus
398 ———— phreniticus
396*———— crassicostatus
397*———— calyculatus
398*———— *squamosus*

c

399 Cardita *squamiferus*
400 ——— *incrassatus*

CYPRICARDIA.

401 Cypricardia Guinaica? oblonga, Sowerby
402 ——— angulata? two beautiful specimens
and one very young
403 ——— rostrata?
403a——— rostrata, var.

ISOCARDIA.

404 Isocardia Cor
405 ——— Moltkiana; two specimens, one of
which is white, the other spotted with pale
fulvous and rose colour; this latter differs in
shape from the other, and agrees precisely
with the figure in Encycl. Meth. t. 233, f. 1

CUCULLÆA.

406 Cucullæa auriculifera

ARCA.

407 Arca tortuosa, several specimens, various sizes
408 ——— Noæ, many specimens, several small groups
409 ——— retusa
410 ——— ovata
411 ——— barbata
412 ——— fusca
413 ——— Helbingii
414 ——— Scapha *(a)* varietas?
415 ——— antiquata; *(a. b.)* varietates
416 ——— rhombea, several specimens; *(a)* var. transversè elongata
417 ——— granosa, three varieties mentioned by Lamarck

418 Arca inæquivalvis
419 —— Indica
420 —— senilis; several specimens, of which one is
enormously large, and one small one a mon-
strosity
421 —— Brasiliensis
422 —— Corbicula

PECTUNCULUS.

423 Pectunculus Glycimeris, several specimens
424 ———— pilosus, several specimens
425 ———— marmoratus
426 ———— scriptus
427 ———— rubens
428 ———— angulatus
429 ———— pectiniformis
430 ———— pectinatus
431 ————
432 ————
433 ————
434 ————
435 ———— decussatus, *Arca decussata, Chemn.*
vii. t. 57, f. 561.

NUCULA.

436 Nucula lanceolata
437 —— margaritacea
438 —— Nicobarica
439 —— Pella
440 —— minuta, *auctorum*

CASTALIA.

441 Castalia ambigua

UNIO.

442 Unio elongatus
442a —— sinuosus
443 —— crassidens
444 —— Peruvianus
445 —— purpuratus
446 —— ovatus *(a)* var. radiis longitudinalibus
447 —— delodon ?
448 —— Pictorum
449 —— corrugatus, two varieties
450 —— luteolus
451 —— marginalis
452 —— Ovalis, Mont.
453 ——
454 ——
455 ——
456 ——
457 ——
458 ——
459 ——
460 ——

HYRIA.

461 Hyria avicularis
462 —— corrugata
463 —— elongata, *Swainson*

ANODON.

464 Anodon sulcatus
465 —— anatinus
466 —— intermedius
467 —— trapezialis, a pair, one valve partly un-
coated and polished
468 —— rubens, one valve
469 —— exoticus, different stages of growth

DIPSAS, Leach.

470 Dipsas plicata, Leach; different sizes, and a
    pearl taken from one

IRIDINA.

471 Iridina exotica, a pair, both valves polished

CHAMA.

472 Chama Lazarus, *(a)* a superb group, with an
    Arca Noæ
473 ———— damicornis
474 ———— gryphoides
475 ———— crenulata
476 ———— florida
477 ———— Limbulus
478 ———— asperella
479 ———— æruginosa
480*a*———— ———— var. pallida, rugosa
480*b*———— ———— the same variety, reverse
481 ———— Arcinella, several specimens, superb
    varieties; *(a)* a specimen attached to a
    Strombus; *(b)* another adhering to a Venus
482 ———— Cristella?

ÆTHERIA.

483 Ætheria elliptica

TRIDACNA.

484 Tridacna Gigas, several specimens
484*a*———— ———— var.
485 ———— elongata, several specimens
486 ———— squamosa, several specimens
487 ———— crocea, *(a)* a young one, of an orange
    colour

HIPPOPUS.

488 Hippopus maculatus; a magnificent series of
nine specimens

MODIOLA.

489 Modiola Papuana
490 ———— Tulipa
491 ———— albicostata, varieties
492 ———— picta
493 ———— sulcata
494 ———— plicatula, *(a)* var. *incurva*
495 ———— semi-fusca? two specimens, each having one valve polished
496 ———— securis
496*a*———— ——— var.
497 ———— discrepans
498 ———— discors; several detached specimens,
and a large group in the byssus
499 ———— trapezina
500 ———— plicata
500*a*————

MYTILUS.

501 Mytilus Magellanicus
502 ———— crenatus, (an merè varietas præcedentis)
503 ———— hirsutus
504 ———— bilocularis, many varieties in shape
505 ———— elongatus, several speeimens
506 ———— latus
507 ———— zonarius, both valves polished
508 ———— ungulatus
509 ———— violaceus
510 ———— Opalus
511 ———— smaragdinus
512 ———— Afer
513 ———— achatinus

514 Mytilus ungularis
515 ———— edulis. *(a. b.)* distortions

PINNA.

516 Pinna rudis
517 ———— Flabellum
518 ———— semi-nuda
519 ———— nobilis
520 ———— squamosa
521 ———— muricata
522 ———— marginata
523 ———— pectinata
524 ———— saccata, several varieties
525 ———— dolabrata, three strong varieties in form
526 ———— inflata, Chemn. VIII. t. 87, f. 772
527 ———— nigrina
528 ———— incurvata, *Chemn.* VIII. t. 90, f. 778
529 ———— bicolor, Chemn. VIII. t. 90, f. 780. rotun-
    data, *Lin?*
530 ———— var.
531 ———— *serrata* (Humphrey.)
531a———— *atro-purpurea*

CRENATULA.

532 Crenatula avicularis
533 ———— nigrina?
534 ———— mytiloides
535 ———— Phasianoptera

PERNA.

536 Perna Ephippium
536a———— ———— var. albida
537 ———— obliqua
538 ———— Isognomum
539 ———— femoralis
540 ———— Marsupium

541 Perna sulcata ?
542 ———
543 ———
544 ———

MALLEUS.

545 Malleus albus
546 ——— vulgaris
547 ——— mormalis
548 ——— anatinus
549 ——— vulsellatus
550 ——— decurtatus

AVICULA.

551 Avicula macroptera
552 ——— semi-sagitta
553 ——— heteroptera
554 ——— falcata
555 ——— crocea
556 ——— Atlantica?
557 ——— squamulosa, several varieties
558 ——— papilionacea, several varieties
559 ——— costellata?
559a——— ———

MELEAGRINA.

560 Meleagrina margaritifera
561 ——————— albina

LIMA.

562 Lima inflata
563 —— squamosa, several specimens
564 —— glacialis
565 —— fragilis
566 —— Linguatula

PECTEN.

567 Pecten maximus
568 ———— medius
569 ———— Jacobæus, many varieties
570 ———— bifrons, two varieties
571 ———— Ziczac
572 ———— Laurentii
573 ———— Pleuronectes, many varieties
574 ———— obliteratus
575 ———— Japonicus
576 ———— Magellanicus
577 ———— Radula
578 ———— Rastellum?
579 ———— turgidus
580 ———— aspersus
581 ———— flavidulus
582 ———— Plica
583 ———— glaber
584 ———— sulcatus
585 ———— Virgo
586 ———— unicolor
587 ———— griseus
588 ———— distans
589 ———— Isabella
590 ———— nodosus
591 ———— Pallium, many varieties
592 ———— Pes-felis
593 ———— Tigris
594 ———— imbricatus
595 ———— histrionicus
596 ———— opercularis
597 ———— Islandicus
598 ———— asperrimus
599 ———— senatorius
600 ———— aurantius
601 ———— varius

602 Pecten sinuosus
603 ———— Pusio
604 ———— hybridus
605 ———— pyxidatus, Ostr. pyxidata, *Dillw.*
606 ———— ornatus
607 ———— Tranquebaricus
608 ———— sanguineus
609 ————
610 ————
611 ————
612 ————
613 ————
614 ————

PLICATULA.

615 Plicatula ramosa
616 ———— cristata

SPONDYLUS.

617 Spondylus Gæderopus, numerous varieties
618 ———— Americanus, numerous and fine varieties
619 ———— arachnoides
620 ———— multilamellatus
621 ———— costatus
622 ———— regius
623 ———— coccineus
623*a* ———— coccineus var. ?
624 ———— crassisquamatus
625 ———— spathuliferus
626 ———— croceus
627 ———— aurantius
628 ———— radians
629 ———— ducalis var. ? testâ croceâ, costis
squamiferis, numerosis, squamis albis

OSTREA.

630 Ostrea Borealis
631 ———— Cochlear
632 ———— cristata
633 ———— Gallina
634 ———— parasitica, one magnificent specimen
635 ———— denticulata
636 ———— Ruscuriana
637 ———— Virginica, several small specimens
638 ———— Canadensis?
639 ———— edulis
640 ———— Cornucopiæ
641 ———— cucullata
642 ———— Limacella
643 ———— Folium
644 ———— Crista-Galli
645 ———— turbinata?
646 ———— imbricata
647 ———— Hyotis
648 ————
649 ————
650 ————
651 ————
652 ————
653 ————
654 ————
655 ————
656 ————
657 ————
658 ————

VULSELLA.

659 Vulsella lingulata, four varieties

PLACUNA.

660 Placuna Sella, several specimens
661 ———— papyracea
662 ———— Placenta

ANOMIA.

663 Anomia Ephippium, one detached and several
    adhering to a stone
664 ———— patellaris
665 ———— ænigmatica, Chemn. xi. t. 199, f. 1949
    1950
666 ———— electrica
667 ———— membranacea

TEREBRATULA.

668 Terebratula vitrea
669 ———— dilatata
670 ———— dorsata
671 ———— Caput-serpentis
672 ———— truncata
673 ———— psittacea
674 ———— dentata
675 ———— rosea, (nonnul.)
676 ———— picta, (Humphrey)

LINGULA.

677 Lingula anatina, one specimen having its pe-
    duncle
678 ———— hians, Swainson in Phil. Mag. vol. 62,
    p. 403

HYALÆA.

679 Hyalæa tridentata
680 ———— rostrata. *Rheda rostrata*, Humphrey MS.

CHITON.

681 Chiton Gigas, two fine specimens
682 ———— squamosus
683 ———— aculeatus, Dillw,
684 ———— fulvus, Id.
685 ———— piceus, Id.
686 ———— granulatus, Id.
687 ———— fasciatus, Id,
688 ———— *tuberculiferus*, (Nobis) *Aculeatus*, Barnes in Amer. Phil. Journal
689 ———— marmoratus, Dillw.
690 ———— sulcatus, Wood
691 ———— amiculatus, Dillw. p. 6
692 ———— *latus*
693 ———— *rugulosus*

PATELLA.

694 Patella Granatum, many varieties in size and colour
695 ———— Oculus, same observation
697 ———— Barbara? several specimens extremely variable in size, one very large
698 ———— laciniosa
699 ———— saccharina
700 ———— longicostata, several specimens
701 ———— spinifera
702 ———— Umbella
703 ———— cærulea, numerous varieties
704 ———— testudinaria, several extremely fine specimens
705 ———— Cochlear
706 ———— radians?
707 ———— compressa, several beautiful varieties; (a) a specimen of extraordinary size, to which several Balani are adhering; (b) a specimen of remarkably fine colour; (c) a specimen showing the identity of *P. compressa* and *miniata*, its vertex being P. miniata and the remainder P. compressa

708 Patella granularis
709 ———— deaurata, many varieties
710 ———— Magellanica
711 ———— stellifera
712 ———— vulgata
713 ———— miniata
714 ———— punctata
715 ———— pectinata
716 ———— puncturata
717 ———— Galatea?
718 ———— tricostata
719 ———— tenuis; Dillw.
720 ———— margaritacea; *Dillw.*
721 ———— pellucida, a large conical variety
722 ———— Cypria, Dillw.
723 ———— ornata, Dillw.
724 ———— Tramoserica, Chemn. xi. t. 197, f. 1912, 1913, many specimens
725 ———— melanogramma, Dillw.
726 ———— tuberculata? Dillw. The Gorgon Limpet from the coast of Barbary, *Budgin* MS. six specimens in different stages of growth
727 ———— radians, Dillw.
728 ———— Rota, Dillw.
729 ———— testudinalis, Dillw. *Clealandi*, J. Sowerby
730 ———— flammea, Dillw.
731 ———— lævigata, Dillw.
732 ———— Surinamensis, Dillw.
733 to 738. These and some of the following cannot be referred with certainty to any described species: we have not, however, ventured to describe them, partly on account of the great variation to which every species is subject, and partly on account of the extreme ambiguity of many of the descriptions and figures already extant.
739 ———— nigra, Budgin MS.
740 ———— plumbea?

741 Patella Cymbularia
742 ——— Jamaicensis ? Dillw.
743 ——— octo-radiata ? Gmel.
744 ——— fragilis, Chemn. xi. t. 197, f. 1921
745 to 772, unnamed for the reason above assigned.

UMBRELLA.

773 Umbrella Indica
774 ——— Mediterranea ?

PARMOPHORUS.

775 Parmophorus Australis, several fine specimens
776 ——— breviculus ?
777 ——— granulatus ?

EMARGINULA.

778 Emarginula notata, *Patella notata*, Linn. Chemn.
x. Vign. 25, f. C. D.
779 ——— aspera, *Patella aspera, Humph. MS.*
780 ——— tricostata
781 ——— reticulata

FISSURELLA.

782 Fissurella picta, many specimens
783 ——— nimbosa
784 ——— Græca
785 ——— nodosa
786 ——— rosea
787 ——— Barbadensis
788 ——— viridula
789 ——— hiantula
790 ——— Pustula
791 ——— fascicularis
792 ——— Javana ?
793 ——— minuta
794 ——— *aperta*

795 Fissurella *clypeiformis*
796 ————— *crenulata*
797 —————
798 —————
799 —————
800 —————
801 —————
802 ————— cancellata, *Solander*

SIPHONARIA, SOWERBYS' Genera of Shells

803 Siphonaria Sipho, several varieties and many
    specimens
804 ————— Mouret; *Mouret, Adanson*
805 ————— concinna
806 ————— Tristensis?
807 ————— exigua
808 ————— *Gigas*
809 ————— *obliquata*

PILEOPSIS.

810 Pileopsis Ungarica
811 ————— Mitrula
812 ————— subrufa
812a————— Cassida, *Patella Cassida*, Dillw.
813 ————— intorta?
813a————— Calyptra, *Patella Calyptra*, Dillw.

CALYPTRÆA.

814 Calyptræa Extinctorium, Sowerbys' Genera of
    Shells, No. 23
815 ————— spinosa, Id.
816 ————— equestris
817 ————— Chinensis
818 ————— Pileus, Nobis; *Trocus Pileus*, Lam.
819 ————— dilatata, Nobis

820 Calyptræa auriculata, Patella auriculata, Dillw.
    many varieties
821 ————— *Comma-notata*
822 ————— radians. *Trochus radians, Lam.*

CREPIDULA.

823 Crepidula fornicata
824 ————— Porcellana
825 ————— aculeata
826 ————— unguiformis
827 ————— dilatata
828 ————— *adunca*

BULLÆA.

829 Bullæa aperta

BULLA.

830 Bulla lignaria
831 ——— Ampulla, a considerable series of fine va-
    rieties in colour and markings
832 ——— striata
833 ——— Naucum
834 ——— Physis, several fine specimens
835 ——— fasciata, several fine specimens, of which
    one is remarkable for being white with four
    fuscous, transverse bands
836 ——— Aplustre, several fine specimens
837 ——— Hydatis
838 ——— solida
839 ——— nitidula, Solander

DOLABELLA.

840 Dolabella Rumphii

OBSERVATION.—*From hence to the end of the Land Shells, we have followed as far as possible the arrangement of De Ferussac.*

HELICARION.

841 Helicarion Cuvieri

HELICOLIMAX.

842 Helicolimax Lamarckii

HELICOPHANTA.

843 Helicophanta Cornu-giganteum. Helix vesicalis, Lam.

COCHLOHYDRA.

844 Cochlohydra putris. Succinea amphibea, Lam.

HELICOGENA.

845 Helicogena naticoides. Helix naticoides, Lam.
846 ———— picta, several beautiful varieties, Helix picta, Lam.
847 ———— Jamaicensis. Helix pulla, Lam.
848 ———— Cornu militare. Helix gigantea, Lam.
849 ———— undulata. Helix lineolata, Lam.
850 ———— crispata ?
851 ———— melanostoma. Helix, Lam.
852 ———— cincta
853 ———— ligata
854 ———— Lucorum. Helix mutata, Lam.
855 ———— Pomatia; *(a)* several reverse spemens; *(b)* one perfect var. scalaris. Helix scalaris, *Mull.*
856 ———— Lucana, *Helix, Lam.*
857 ———— Globulus, *Helix, Lam.*

858 Helicogena Prunum
859 ————— vittata, *Helix, Lam.*
860 ————— argillacea, *Helix, Lam.*
861 ————— Arbustorum, *Helix, Lam.*
862 ————— maculosa, *Helix, Lam.*
863 ————— Cœlatura, *Helix, Lam.*
864 ————— Otaheitana
864*a* ————————— var. superne pallidior
865 ————— candidissima, *Helix, Lam.*
866 ————— aspersa, Helix, *Lam.*
867 ————— hæmastoma, *Helix, Lam.*
868 ————— malanotragus, *Helix, Lam.*
869 ————— nemoralis, Helix, **Lam.**
870 ————— hortensis, Id.
871 ————— vermicularis, Id.
872 ————— marmorata
873 ————— serpentina? Id.
874 ————— Pouchet
875 ————— albilabris
876 ————— aspera
877 ————— lactea, *Helix, Lam.* many varieties
878 ————— auricoma, Helix microstoma, Lam.
879 ————— Lima, Helix punctifera, Lamarck,
    (a) variety
880 ————— formosa
881 ————— Carmelita
882 ————— orbiculata
883 ————— auriculata

HELICODON.

884 Helicodon Thyroidus
885 ——— denotatus
886 ——— septemvolutus. H. Septemvolva, De
    Fer. *Helix, planorbula, Lam.*
886*b* ——— Epistyllum, Helix Cookiana, Lam.
887 ——— ringens, *Anostoma depressa, Lam.*
888 ——— ringiculus, ——— *globulosa, Lam.*

889 Helicodon Cepa *Helix, Lam.*
890 ——— sinuatus et sinuosus, *Helix, Lam.* *(a, b, c)* different varieties
891 ——— Soror
892 ——— Lamarckii ; *(a)* Carocolla acutissima, Lam.; *(b)* Helix heteroclites, Lam.
892a ———

HELICIGONA.

893 Helicigona angistoma, *Carocolla, Lam.*
894 ——— Carocolla, *Carocolla albilabris,* Lam.
895 ——— inversicolor, ——— *bicolor,* Lam.
896 ——— obliterata, ——— *inflata,* Lam.
897 ——— Gualteriana, *Carocolla,* Lam.
898 ——— Lampas
899 ——— pyrostoma
900 ——— marginata, several varieties, *Carocolla, Lam.*
901 ——— Pileus, *Helix, Lam.*
902 ——— scabrosa

HELICELLA.

903 Helicella zonata
904 ——— zonalis var.
905 ——— Exceptiuncula var.
906 ——— zonaria
907 ——— Madecassina, *Helix Madagascariensis, Lam.*
908 ——— sepulchralis, *Helix, Lam.*
909 ——— zodiacus
910 ——— Pellis-Serpentis, *Helix, Lam.*
911 ——— Senegalensis, *Helix, Lam.* three young and three full grown specimens
912 ——— Unguiculus, *(a, b)* distinct varieties
913 ——— Ungulina, *Helix, ungulina, Lam.*
914 ——— Algira, Helix, Lam.
915 ——— lævipes, Helix, Lam.

916 Helicella exilis
917 ———— unizonalis, Helix monozonalis, Lam.
918 ———— citrina, Helix, *Lam.* numerous varieties
919 ———— Clairvillii
920 ———— Carthusianella, Helix, Lam.
921 ———— Fruticum, Id.
922 ———— Ericetorum, Id.
923 ———— Cespitum, Id.
924 ———— Pisana, Id.
925 ———— bipartita
926 ———— ————
926a ———— ————
927 ———— ————
928 ———— ————
929 ———— ————
929a ———— ————
930 ———— ————
930a ———— ————
931 ———— *Helix tessellata, Budgin* MS.
932 ———— ————
933 ———— ———— from New South Wales
934 ———— *Helix producta, Budgin,* from Canton
935 ———— *Helix pallida, Budgin,* from Virginia
936 ————

COCHLOSTYLA.

937 Cochlostyla Pythogaster, Bulimus, Lam.
938 ———— Dufresnii
939 ———— Taunaisii? one full grown and one young specimen
940 ———— Pardalis
941 ———— Peruviana, Bulimus, Lam.
942 ———— undata, Bulimus, Lam. several specimens
943 ———— Sultana, *Bulimus* Gallina Sultana, Lam. two specimens of great beauty, one of them enormously large
944 ————
945 ————

COCHLITOMA.

946 Cochlitoma exarata
947 ———— flammigera, two varieties
948 ———— Regina; *(a, b, c, d)* Achatina melastoma, Sw. *(e)* the same reverse. *Achatina perversa, Sw.*
949 ———— virginea, numerous and brilliant varieties
950 ———— Vexillum; Achatina Vexillum, *Lam.* *(a)* Ach. fasciata, Sw. *(b)* Ach. crenata, Sw. *(c)* Ach. fasciata, Sw. but possessing the green lines of Ach. crenata, Sw. therefore intermediate. *(d)* Ach. pallida, Sw. *(e)* var. immaculata, fasciis luteis pallidis
Obs. Of this species the Collection exhibits a numerous and magnificent series of varieties.
951 ———— vittata, Nobis, *Achatina vittata, Sw.* one reverse specimen
952 ———— Fulica?
953 ———— bicarinata; *(a)* varietas, lineis tribus albidis, interruptis
954 ———— purpurea, Achatina purpurea, Lam. several specimens and vareties
955 ———— achatina, Achatina Perdix, Lam. six specimens with and six without the epidermis
956 ———— Zebra, *Achatina,* Lam. several specimens
957 ———— marginata, Achatina marginata, Sw. three specimens, of which one is extraordinarily large
958 ———— purpurea, var.
959 ———— Fulica, var.?

COCHLICOPA.

960 Cochlicopa Priamus, Achatina, Lam.
961 ———— rosea, *(a)* var. elongata
962 ———— Glans, Achatina, Lam.

963 Cochlicopa leucozonias, Achatina albolineata,
　　Lam.
964 ——————— Columna, Achatina, Lam.
964a——————— octona

COCHLICELLA.

965 Cochlicella decollata, Bulimus decollatus, Lam.

COCHLOGENA.

966 Cochlogena flammata
967 ——————— Kambeul, Bulimus, Lam.
968 ——————— flammea, *Achatina ustulata? Lam.*
969 ——————— radiata, Bulimus, Lam.
970 ——————— Guadaloupensis, Bulimus, Lamarck
　　(a) var. monstrosa
971 ——————— virgulata, Bulimus Caribæorum,
　　Lam.
972 ——————— liliacea ?
973 ——————— *maxima*
974 ——————— ovata; *(a)* testâ junior; *(b)* var.
　　elongata; *(c)* var. ovoidea
975 ——————— oblonga, *Bulimus hæmastomus,* Lam.
976 ——————— aurea, *Bulimus citrinus et inversus,*
　　Lam.; *(a)* testâ sinistrorsâ, many varieties;
　　(b) testâ dextrâ, many varieties
977 ——————— interrupta, (sinistrorsa) Bulimus,
　　Lam. many specimens
977a——————— læva
978 ——————— trizonalis, *Bulimus zonatus,* Sw.
979 ——————— decora
980 ——————— lugubris
981 ——————— Auris-Leporis
982 ——————— Auris-Sileni, *Carychium undulatum,*
　　Leach.
983 ——————— goniostoma
984 ——————— Auris-caprina, *Auricula Auris-Sileni,*
　　Lam.

985 Cochlogena distorta
986 ———————— Auris-vulpina
987 ———————— Auris-bovina, two varieties

COCHLODON.

988 Cochlodon Uva
989 ————— Mumia
990 ————— sulcatus
991 ————— Lyonetianus
992 ————— cinereus

COCHLODINA.

993 Cochlodina tortuosa, from Tranquebar
994 ——————— Cylindrus
995 ——————— Chemnitziana
996 ——————— papillaris

PARTULA.

997 Partula pudica
997a ———— *unidentata*
998 ———— Australis
999 ———— gibba?
1000 ———— Otaheitana
1000a ———— ———— var.

SCARABUS.

1001 Scarabus Imbrium
1002 ————— plicatus

AURICULA.

1003 Auricula Midæ, several specimens
1004 ————— Judæ
1005 ————— Auricella
1006 ————— Felis
1007 ————— Nucleus
    Obs. From this place we resume the nomen-
    clature of Lamarck

CYCLOSTOMA.

1008 Cyclostoma Volvulus, many specimens
1008a——— ——— an varietas? several specimens
1009 ——— unicarinatum
1010 ——— ligatum
1011 ——— elegans
1012 ——— foliaceum, Turbo foliaceus, Dillw.
1013 ——— Jamaicense, Turbo Jamaicensis, Chemn. xi. t. 209, f. 2057, 2058
1014 ——— fimbriatum, Turbo fimbriatus, Budgin MS. (not Cyclost. fimbriata, Lam.)
1015 ——— *fimbriatulum*
1016 ——— *unifasciatum*
1017 ——— striatum, Turbo striatus, Budgin MS.
1018 ——— subrufum, Turbo subrufus, Id.
1019 ———
1020 ———
1021 ———

HELICINA, (Gray, in Zoological Journal.)

1022 Helicina pulchella
1023 ——— Brownii
1024 ——— Maugeriæ?
1025 ——— *Tankervillii*, Gray, in Zool. Journal, vol. i.—*Obs.* In general form this species resembles H. pulchella, *Gray;* it is, however, much larger, and distinguished moreover by its strongly crenulated sharp keel. Locality not known.

PLANORBIS.

1026 Planorbis corneus var.; from Nova Scotia
1027 ——— carinatus, from Tranquebar
1028 ——— Guadaloupensis

PHYSA.

1029 Physa castanea
1030 ———— fontinalis var.? from Canada
1031 ———— rivalis, *Helix, Maton and Rackett*

LIMNÆA.

1032 Limnæa stagnalis
1033 ———— palustris var.? from Canada. An fortius, L. Virginiana, *Lam.?*
1034 ———— rufescens, *Gray*. See Sowerbys' Genera of Shells, an L. acuminata? Lam.
1035 ———— auricularia
1036 ———— *Timorensis*
1037 ———— Pacifica, *Helix Pacifica, Budgin* MS. From the South Sea Islands
1038 ———— corrugata, *Helix corrugata, Budgin* MS. From Georgia
1039 ———— *subglobosa*

MELANIA.

1040 Melania punctata
1041 ———— subulata?
1042 ———— decollata
1043 ———— lævigata? From the Matavai River, Otaheite
1044 ———— amarula, *(a)* decorticata, *(b)* spirâ breviore, spinis majusculis, paucis
1045 ———— setosa, Sw.
1046 ———— spinulosa
1047 ———— carinifera?
1048 ———— truncatula?
1048a———— *inermis*
1049 ————
1050 ————
1051 ————
1052 ————
1053 ————
1054 ————

43

MELANOPSIS.

1055 Melanopsis lævigata
1056 ———— *labiata*

PIRENA.

1057 Pirena terebralis, several specimens, one of
     them young
1058 ——— spinosa
1059 ——— aurita
1059a——— an merè P. auritæ testæ juniores? an
     species distincta?
1060 ——— sinuata, *Buccinum sinuatum, Dillw.*

PALUDINA.

1061 Paludina vivipara
1062 ——— an var. P. viviparæ, sine fasciis?
     P. unicolor, Sw.
1063 ——— Bengalensis, P. elongata, Sw. Zool.
     Illus.
1064 ——— unicolor
1065 ——— carinata, Swainson Illus.
1066 ——— impura
1067 ——— parva, *Helix parva, Budgin* MS. from
     Danes Island
1068 ——— *viridis,* Helix viridata, Budgin MS.
     from Virginia
1069 ——— *olivacea*
1070 ——— *bicolor*

AMPULLARIA.

1071 Ampullaria Cornu—Arietis, Sowerbys' Genera
     of Shells. *Planorbis, Lam.*
1072 ——— Guyanensis, A. globosa, Sw. Illus.
1073 ——— rugosa
1074 ——— fasciata, Lam. and Sw. Zool. Ill.
1074a——— fasciata var. Sw. in Bligh Catalogue

1075 Ampullaria fasciata var. monstrosa
1076a——————— canaliculata? spirâ erosâ
1076 ——————— effusa, many varieties
1077 ——————— carinata, Sw. (not of Lam.)
1078 ——————— Avellana; undoubtedly a marine
　　　 shell, as Bruguière suspected, notwithstand-
　　　 ing Lamarck's assertion that it is a river shell
1079 ——————— intorta
1080 ——————— chlorostoma, *A. luteostoma*, Swain.
　　　 A. effusa, De Fer. MS.
1081 ——————— oblonga, Swain. Zool. Ill.
1082 ——————— reflexa, Swain. Zool. Ill.
1083 ——————— corrugata, Swain. Zool. Ill.
1084 ——————— sordita? Swain. Zool. Ill.
1085 ———————
1086 ——————— ——————— not umbilicated, it never-
　　　 theless appears to be distinct from Swainson's
　　　 A. crassa
1087 ———————
1088 ———————
1089 ——————— *megastoma*

NAVICELLA.

1090 Navicella elliptica
1091 ——————— tessellata, from Timor and Sumatra
1092 ——————— *suborbicularis*

NERITINA.

1093 Neritina pulligera, *(a)* from Tranquebar; *(b)*
　　　 from the Nicobar Islands
1094 ——————— *Canalis*
1095 ——————— dubia
1096 ——————— Zebra
1097 ——————— Zigzag
1098 ——————— Gagates, from Sumatra
1099 ——————— lugubris?

1100 Neritina Corona
1101 ———— brevispinosa
1102 ———— *spinosa, Budgin* MS. Species N. coronæ valdè affinis, sed magis elongata, spinis
brevibus, epidermide viridi-fescâ, strigis ni-
gris. From Otaheite. An potius varietas
N. Coronæ?
1103 ———— crepidularia. Nerita purpurea, Budgin, from Tranquebar, *(a)* var. from Danes
Island, Wampoa, N. gracilenta, Budgin
1104 ———— auriculata, Sumatra
1105 ———— Domingensis?
1106 ———— fasciata, *(a)* varietates?
1107 ———— semiconica
1108 ———— strigilata; several specimens from
Sumatra
1109 ———— Meleagris
1110 ———— Virginea
1111 ———— viridis
1112 ———— punctulata, *De Ferussao,* Nerita aperta, Budg.
1113 ———— Pupa, Nerita Pupa, Dillw.
1114 ———— reticulata, Nerita reticulata, Budgin.
An varietas N. virgineæ
1115 ———— *granosa*
1116 ————
1117 ———— ———— from China
1118 ———— ———— from Tranquebar
1119 ————

NERITA.

1120 Nerita Exuvia
1121 ——— textilis
1122 ——— ornatus
1123 ——— Peloronta
1124 ——— Chlorostoma?
1125 ——— atratus

1126 Nerita politus, numerous varieties; *(a)* testâ
transversim striatâ; *(b)* ore aurantiaco
1127 ——— albicillus
1128 ——— Chamæleon
1129 ——— versicolor
1130 ——— Ascensionis
1131 ——— Mallaccensis?
1131*a*——— lineatus
1132 ——— scabricostatus
1133 ——— plicatus
1134 ——— tessellatus
1135 ——— Antillarum, Dillw. (Chemn. v. t 192.
f. 1987.)
1136 ——— undatus
1136*a*——— ——— var.
1137 ——— maximus? Dillw.
1138 ——— ——— I believe this to be undescribed,
but the characters of most of the species are
so vague that it cannot be ascertained at present. From the Nicobar Islands.
1139 ———

NATICA.

1140 Natica glaucina
1141 ——— Albumen
1142 ——— mammillaris
1143 ——— Mammilla
1144 ——— melanostoma
1145 ——— aurantiaca
1146 ——— conica
1147 ——— plumbea
1148 ——— Canrena, many specimens and varieties
1149 ——— cruentata
1150 ——— millepunctata
1151 ——— Vitellus
1152 ——— helvacea, N. spadicea, Swainson
1153 ——— rufa
1154 ——— unifasciata?

1155 Natica lineata
1156 ———— fulminea, and varieties
1157 ———— Marochiensis
1158 ———— arachnoidea
1159 ———— Zebra
1160 ———— Chinensis
1161 ———— cancellata
1162 ———— Maura, Encycl. 453, f. 4.
1163 ———— collaris, Nerita collaris ornata, &c. Chemn. v, t. 187, f. 1895, *a* and *b*
1164 ———— Orientalis B. Dillw.; *eburnea*, Chemn. v. 188, f. 1904
1165 ———— Maroccana, Chemn. v. t. 188, f. 1909, 1910
1166 ———— glaucina of British Authors
1167 ———— an varietas N. millepunctatæ?
1168 ———— Forskälii, Chemn. xi. t. 197, f. 1901, 1902
1169 ———— duplicata, Say
1170 ———— *violacea*, Budgin MS.
1171 ———— effusa, Swainson; varietates absque maculis castaneis
1172 ———— ————
1173 ———— ———— from Ceylon
1174 ———— nebulosa, Nerita nebulosa, Budgin. The painted breast Snail from China
1175 ———— marmorata, Nerita marmorata, Budg.
1176 ———— torquata, Nerita, Budgin
1177 ———— maculata, Nerita, *Ulysses*, according to Dillwyn, who ranks this as a var. of N. canrena, Chemn. v. t. 187, f. 1876 to 1880; *(a)* var. notabilis, Nerita tessellata, Budgin; *(b)* var. lineato-maculata
1178 ———— nigra. Nerita nigrata, Budgin
1179 ———— *fluctuata*
1180 ————
1181 ————
1182 ————

IANTHINA.

1183 Ianthina communis, many specimens
1184 ———— globosa, Swain.
1185 ———— exigua

SIGARETUS.

1186 Sigaretus haliotoideus
1187 ———— concavus
1188 ———— Leachii, Cryptostoma Leachii, De
    Blain.
1189 ———— cancellatus

STOMATELLA.

1190 Stomatella imbricata
1191 ———— sulcifera
1192 ———— auricula
1193 ———— planulata

STOMATIA.

1194 Stomatia Phimotis
1195 ———— duplicata
1196 ———— obscurata

HALIOTIS.

1197 Haliotis Midæ
1198 ———— Iris
1199 ———— tubifera
1200 ———— excavata
1201 ———— Australis
1202 ———— tuberculata
1203 ———— striata ?
1204 ———— asinina
1205 ———— glabra
1206 ———— lamellosa

1207 Haliotis
1208 ———— tricostalis, two remarkably fine specimens
1209 ———— pulcherrima, Dillw.
1210 ———— virginea, Dillw.
1211 ———— varia, Dillw.
1212 ———— gigantea, Dillw.
1213 ———— Cracherodii, Leach
1214 ———— Californiensis, Swains.
1215 ————
1216 ————
1217 ————
1218 ————
1219 ————
1220 ————
1221 ————
1222 ————
1223 ————
1224 ————
1225 ————
1226 ————

TORNATELLA.

1227 Tornatella flammea
1228 ———— solidula
1229 ———— fasciata
1230 ———— nitidula
1231 ———— solidula var.

PYRAMIDELLA.

1232 Pyramidella Terebellum
1233 ———— dolabrata
1234 ———— plicata
1235 ———— maculosa
1235a ———— maculosa var. nebulosa
1236 ———— solida

G

SCALARIA.

1237 Scalaria pretiosa
1238 ───── coronata
1239 ───── varicosa
1240 ───── communis
1241 ───── raricostata
1242 ───── principalis, Turbo principalis,
    Chemn. iv. t. 152, f. 1428
1243 ───── Clathratulus, Turbo clathratulus,
    auctorum
1244 ─────
1245 ─────
1246 ─────
1247 ─────

DELPHINULA.

1248 Delphinula laciniata, many fine specimens
1248a───── ───── a singularly distorted
    specimen
1249 ───── distorta
1250 ───── trigonostoma

RISSOA

De Blainv. Dict. des Sciences nat. article Mollusques.

1250aRissoa acuta
1251 ───── labiosa, Turbo labiosus, Mont.
1252 ───── parva, Turbo parvus, Mont.
1253 ───── striata, Turbo striatus, Mont.

SOLARIUM.

1254 Solarium perspectivum
1255 ───── granulatum
1256 ───── lævigatum
1257 ───── stramineum
1258 ───── hybridum
1259 ───── variegatum

ROTELLA.

1260 Rotella lineolata, and rosea, very numerous
    varieties

TROCHUS.

1261 Trochus imperialis, several specimens
1262 ———— longispinosus
1263 ———— solaris
1264 ———— Indicus
1265 ———— brevispinosus ?
1266 ———— stellaris
1267 ———— rhodostomus
1268 ———— inermis
1269 ———— agglutinans
1270 ———— cælatus
1271 ———— Tuber
1272 ———— Magus
1273 ———— Merula
1274 ———— argyrostomus
1275 ———— Cookii
1276 ———— Niloticus
1277 ———— pyramidalis
1278 ———— noduliferus
1279 ———— cærulescens
1280 ———— Obeliscus
1281 ———— virgatus
1282 ———— maculatus
1283 ———— squarrosus
1284 ———— incrassatus
1285 ———— flammulatus ?
1286 ———— elatus, *Trochus Conus, Dillw.*
1287 ———— Mauritianus
1288 ———— imbricatus
1289 ———— concavus
1290 ———— ziziphinus
1291 ———— Conulus
1292 ———— jujubinus

1293 Trochus annulatus
1294 ———— doliarius; *(a)* a specimen with a
　　　 Crepidula attached
1295 ———— granulatus
1296 ———— Grapatum
1297 ———— Iris
1298 ———— calliferus, from Ceylon
1299 ———— undatus
1300 ———— Pharaonis, several varieties
1301 ———— excavatus
1302 ———— Carneolus
1303 ———— erythroleucos?
1304 ———— dentatus var. Dillw.
1305 ———— undulatus
1306 ———— ———— New Zealand
1307 ———— ———— Ditto
1308 ———— ———— Tranquebar
1309 ———— ———— King George's Sound
1310 ————
1311 ————
1312 ————
1313 ————
1314 ————
1315 ————
1316 ———— regius, Dillw.
1317 ————
1318 ————
1319 ————
1320 ————
1321 ————
1322 ————
1323 ————
1324 ————
1325 ————
1326 ————
1327 ————
1328 ————
1329 ————

1330 Trochus
1331 ————————
1332 ————————
1333 ————————
1334 ————————
1335 ————————
1336 ————————

ODONTIS*.

1337 Odontis   Pagodus
1338 ———————— Tectum Persicum
1339 ———————— coronaria
1340 ———————— Ægyptiaca
1341 ———————— Modulus
1342 ———————— Tectum
1343 ———————— Labeo
1344 ———————— Australis
1345 ———————— fragarioides
1346 ———————— constricta
1347 ———————— canaliculata
1348 ———————— sulcata, Turbo sulcatus, Budgin
1349 ————————
1350 ————————
1351 ————————
1352 ————————
1353 ———————— nigra, Trochus niger, Budgin
1354 ———————— nigrescens, Trochus nigrescens, Id.
1355 ———————— reticulata, Trochus reticulatus, Id.
1356 ———————— marmorata, ———— marmoratus, Id.
1357 ————————
1358 ———————— maculosa, ———— maculosus, Id.
1359 ————————
1360 ————————
1361 ———————— variegata, ———— variegatus, Id.
1362 ———————— virescens, ———— virescens, Id.

* Altered from Monodonta, which every Greek Scholar will perceive
to be inadmissible.

1363 Odontis

1364 ———————

1364*a*——————— rosea

1364*b*——————— ——— from the South Seas

TURBO.

1365 Turbo marmoratus

1366 ——— imperialis

1367 ——— torquatus

1368 ——— Sarmaticus, in various stages of growth

1369 ——— cornutus

1370 ——— argyrostomus, in various stages and
    varieties

1371 ——— chrysostomus, ditto

1372 ——— radiatus

1373 ——— margaritaceus

1374 ——— setosus

1375 ——— Spenglerianus

1376 ——— petholatus, very numerous and beauti-
    ful varieties

1377 ——— undulatus

1378 ——— Pica

1379 ——— versicolor

1380 ——— Smaragdus

1381 ——— Cidaris

1382 ——— diaphanus

1383 ——— rugosus, in various stages of growth

1383*a*——— rugosus, var. muticus

1384 ——— coronatus; *(a)* umbilicatus, umbilico
    parvo

1385 ——— crenulatus? an potiùs species distincta?

1386 ——— Hippocastanum

1387 ——— muricatus

1388 ——— littoreus

1389 ——— ustulatus

1390 ——— Nicobaricus

1391 ——— neritoides

Turbo aculeatus, Dillw.

———— zigzag, *Maton and Rackett*

———— rugosus, var.? Cochlea lunaris rubi-
cunda, &c. Chemn. v. t. 181, f.1803, 1804

———— an varietas, T. setosi, No. 1374? an
Turbo Cochlus, Dillw.

———— cærulescens, Lam.

————

————

————

————

———— *bicarinatus*

———— *tæniatus*

————

————

————

———— niger, T. nigratus, Budgin MS.

————

————

————

————

————

PLANAXIS.

Planaxis undulatus, Bucc. porphyrium, Solander MS.

———— semisulcatus, Sowerbys' Genera of
Shells

———— mollis, Id.

———— sulcatus

———— lineatus, Bucc. lineatum auct.

———— *planicostatus*

PHASIANELLA.

Phasianella bulimoides, about 50 magnificent
varieties

Phasianella rubens

——————— variegata, several remarkably beautiful varieties

——————— Pullus, *Turbo Pullus*, Lam.

——————— Peruviana

——————— angulifera, numerous varieties, *Turbo Porphyrius, Solander* MS.

———————

———————

———————

———————

———————

———————

———————

——————— *reticulata*, Turbo reticulatus, Budg. MS.

TURRITELLA.

Turritella duplicata

——————— Terebra, (Turbo Achimedis, Dillw.) several fine specimens, of which one measures $6\frac{1}{8}$ inches in length : it has 33 volutions

——————— imbricata

——————— replicata

——————— bicingulata

——————— exoleta

——————— *cingulata*

——————————— Turbo Terebra, Dillw.

——————— obsoleta, *Turbo obsoletus?* Dillw.

——————— *cingulifera*

———————

———————

———————

———————

——————— striata, Turbo striatus, Budg. MS.

———————

——————— *spirata*

CERITHIUM.

1450 Cerithium palustre
1451 ———————— sulcatum
1452 ———————— Telescopium
1453 ———————— ebeninum
1454 ———————— nodulosum
1455 ———————— vulgatum
1456 ———————— Obeliscus
1457 ———————— granulatum, Martini, ɪv. t. 157
    f. 1492
1458 ———————— Aluco
1459 ———————— Erythræum?
1460 ———————— muricatum
1461 ———————— asperum; *(a)* varietas
1462 ———————— lineatum
1463 ———————— Vertagus
1463a———————— ———————— var. Martini, ɪv. t. 156,
    f. 1479
1464 ———————— fasciatum
1465 ———————— tuberculatum
1466 ———————— Clava, *Murex Clava, Dillw.*
1467 ————————
1468 ————————
1469 ———————— granulatum, Encycl. Meth. t. 442,
    f. 4
1470 ————————
1471 ————————
1472 ————————
1473 ————————
1474 ————————
1475 ————————
1476 ————————
1477 ————————
1478 ————————
1479 ————————
1480 ————————
1481 ————————

H

1482 Cerithium
1483 —————————
1484 —————————
1485 —————————
1486 —————————
1487 —————————
1488 —————————

PLEUROTOMA.

1489 Pleurotoma muricata
1490 ————— interrupta?
1491 ————— cincta?
1492 ————— Virgo
1493 ————— Babylonica
1494 ————— undosa
1495 ————— marmorata
1496 ————— tigrina
1497 ————— nodifera
1498 ————— cingulifera
1499 ————— Australis, Murex Turris australis, Chemn. x. t.190, f. 1827 1828
1500 ————— gibbosa, Murex gibbosus, Dillw.
1501 ————— an P. muricatæ var.? an potiùs species distincta?
1502 ————— fascialis
1503 ————— *cryptorrhaphe*
1504 ————— lincata, two pale coloured, but very large specimens
1505 —————
1506 —————
1507 —————
1508 —————
1509 —————
1510 ————— Taxus, Chemn. x. t. 162, f. 1550, 1551.—*Obs.* There can be no doubt that Chemnitz's shell is an accidental variety of this shell

1511 Pleurotoma Javanus, Murex Javanus, Linnæi,
     Chemn. iv. t. 143, f. 1336 to 1338

TURBINELLA.

1512 Turbinella Scolymus
1513 ——————— Rapa; *(a)* testâ sinistrorsâ
1514 ——————— Napus
1515 ——————— Pyrum
1516 ——————— pugillaris
1517 ——————— Rhinoceros
1518 ——————— cornigera
1519 ——————— Ceramica
1520 ——————— Capitellum
1521 ——————— Globulus
1522 ——————— rustica
1523 ——————— cingulifera
1524 ——————— polygona
1525 ——————— carinifera
1526 ——————— Infundibulum
1527 ——————— craticulata
1528 ——————— lineata
1529 ——————— Aplustre, *Murex amplustre*, Chemn.
     xi. t. 191, f. 1841, 1842. *The American Flag*
     Buccinum, Martin.
1530 ——————— prismatica, Murex prismaticus,
     Dillw.
1531 ——————— Nassatula?
1532 ——————— ocellata
1533 ——————— *chlorostoma*
1534 ——————— fasciata, Mur. fasciatus, Budg. MS.
1535 ——————— *Fusus*
1535a———————

CANCELLARIA.

1536 Cancellaria reticulata
1537 ——————— scalarina
1538 ——————— cancellata

1539 Cancellaria senticosa
1540 ———— Citharella, Bucc. Alauda, Soland. MS.
1541 ———— elegans, *Sowerbys' Genera of Shells*
1542 ———— an varietas?
1543 ———— *oblonga*
1544 ———— *nodulifera*

FASCIOLARIA.

1545 Fasciolaria Tulipa, many fine varieties
1546 ———— distans
1547 ———— Trapezium
1548 ———— aurantiaca
1549 ———— filamentosa
1550 ———— coronata?
1551 ———— an varietas, F. Trapezii? lineis coloratis obsoletis, magnitudine giganteà; (a) testâ junior
1552 ———— *papillosa*
1553 ———— *Princeps*
1554 ———— an varietas F. aurantiacæ? an species distincta?

FUSUS.

1555 Fusus colosseus; (a) with its epidermis; (b) with its point accidentally distorted
1556 —— longissimus
1557 —— Colus; (a) with a singularly distorted canal
1558 —— tuberculatus
1559 —— Nicobaricus
1560 —— distans?
1560a—— an varietas, F. Nicobarici? an species distincta?
1561 —— torulosus.—*Obs.* There are no specimens precisely according with the description or figure of this shell, in the collection; we sus-

pect, however, that the shells we have marked
1558, Fusus tuberculatus, belong rather to
this species, if indeed it be distinct.

1562 Fusus incrassatus
1563 —— carinatus
1564 —— proboscidiferus, Fusus Aruanus, Swains.
Exot. Conch.
1565 —— Islandicus
1566 —— Morio. This and the following shell are
obviously varieties of the the same species,
though separated by Lamarck.
1567 —— coronatus
1568 —— Corona
1569 —— filosus
1570 —— verruculatus
1571 —— lignarius
1572 —— Syracusanus
1573 —— Cochlidium
1574 —— Antiquus
1575 —— Raphanus
1576 —— sinistralis
1577 —— Nifat
1578 —— articulatus
1579 —— contrarius
1580 ——
1581 ——
1582 —— cariniferus? Encycl. Meth. t. 423, f. 3
1583 ——
1584 ——
1585 ——
1586 ——
1587 ——
1588 ——
1589 ——
1590 ——
1591 ——
1592 ——
1593 ——

1594 Fusus
1595 ———
1596 ———
1597 ———
1598 ———
1598 ———
1599 ———
1600 ———
1601 ———

PYRULA.

1602 Pyrula canaliculata
1603 ——— Carica
1604 ——— perversa
1605 ——— Candelabrum
1606 ——— Tuba, two varieties
1607 ——— bucephala
1608 ——— Vespertilio
1609 ——— Melongena
1610 ——— ——— var. mutica
1611 ——— ——— ——— fusco-nigricans.
     An species distincta?
1612 ——— reticulata
1613 ——— Ficus
1614 ——— *ventricosa*, Chemn. iii. t. 66, f. 733
1615 ——— *gracilis*
1616 ——— ficoides
1617 ——— spirata
1618 ——— Ternatana
1619 ——— Bezoar
1620 ——— Rapa
1621 ——— ——— var. foliacea
1622 ——— papyracea
1623 ——— Galeodes
1624 ——— angulata
1625 ——— nodosa
1626 ——— citrina
1627 ——— squamosa var.?

1628 Pyrula neritoidea
1628*b* ———— Spirillus
1629 ——— *coarctata*, Nobis
1630 ——— ———— testâ sinistrorsâ
1631 ———

STRUTHIOLORIA.

1632 Struthiolaria nodulosa
1633 ———————— inermis, Sowerbys' Genera of
Shells
1634 ———————— *oblita*

RANELLA.

1635 Ranella gigantea
1636 ——— leucostoma, several specimens, one with
its epidermis
1636*a* ——— ———— var. ultimo anfractu tuberculis seriebus duabus cincto
1637 ——— Argus
1638 ——— Crumena.   One specimen only has the
orange red aperture mentioned by Lam.   We
are strongly inclined to suspect that the others
form a distinct species: they are marked
1638 *a.*
1638*b* ——— Crumena.—*Obs.*   The two specimens
bearing this number appear to be a distinct
variety of the last, in which the tubercles on
the varices are lengthened into spines: it has
not the depressed appearance of R. spinosa.
1639 ——— spinosa; *(a)* var. spinâ superiore varicis
dichotomâ
1640 ——— bufonia, *(a)* var. ore fusco
1641 ——— *verrucosa*
1642 ——— granifera
1643 ——— bitubercularis
1644 ——— Gyrinus, Murex Gyrinus, Linn. Ranella
ranina, Lam.
1645 ——— *pulchella*

MUREX.

1646 Murex cornutus; *(a)* triplici cornuum serie
1647 ———— Brundaris
1648 ———— crassispinosus
1649 ———— tenuispinosus
1650 ———— rarispinosus
1651 ———— ternispinosus
1652 ———— brevispinosus
1653 ———— Haustellum
1654 ———— inflatus. Notwithstanding Lamarck's
    opinion that this and the following are distinct,
    we cannot at present decide to which of them
    many specimens belong.
1655 ———— elongatus
1656 ———— Palma-Rosæ
1657 ———— Calcitrapa
1658 ———— adustus
1659 ———— rufus
1660 ———— Axicornis
1661 ———— cervicornis
1662 ———— microphyllus
1663 ———— Capucinus
1664 ———— asperrimus
1665 ———— acanthopterus
1666 ———— tripterus
1667 ———— fimbriatus, Swainson in Bligh Cata-
    logue
1668 ———— uncinarius
1669 ———— gibbosus
1670 ———— triqueter
1671 ———— saxatilis
1672 ———— Brassica
1673 ———— regius, Swainson's Exot. Conch.
1674 ———— Endivia; *(a)* varietas notabilis
1675 ———— Radix
1676 ———— an varietas M. saxatilis, Lam.
1677 ———— melanamathos

1678 Murex hexagonus
1679 ———— Scorpio
1680 ———— secundus
1681 ———— turbinatus, numerous varieties
1682 ———— anguliferus; *(a)* tuberculi spinoso-
muricatis, spinis recurvis; *(b)* spinis recurvis, serratis.
1583 ———— Melonulas
1684 ———— Magellanicus
1685 ———— lamellosus
1686 ———— Erinaceus
1687 ———— scaber?
1688 ———— costularis?
1689 ———— vitulinus
1690 ———— crispatus
1691 ———— fenestratus
1692 ———— concatenatus
1693 ———— Brandaris, Dillw. var.
1694 ———— Scorpio, var. albus; M. Rota, *nonnull.*
(a) frondibus dilatatis brevissimis; *(b)* frondibus dilatatis longioribus; *(c)* frondibus dilatatis
longis, spirâ breviore; *(d)* testa junior.
1695 ———— an varietas M. brevispinosi
1696 ———— an varietas M. Palma-Rosæ
1697 ————
1698 ————
1699 ————
1700 ———— Erinaceus, Encycl. Meth. 421. f. 1?
1701 ———— an var. M. Trunculi?
1702 ———— an var. M. Brassicæ?
1703 ———— *Monodon*, Martini, iii. t. 105, f. 987-8
1704 ———— *Monodon* var.
1705 ———— an spec. nov. from the South Seas?
1706 ———— an spec. nov. from Tranquebar?
1707 ———— an var. Muricis elongati?

TRITON.

1708 Triton variegatus
1709 ——— nodiferus
1710 ——— Australis: (a) monstrum
1711 ——— Lampas
1712 ——— Scrobiculator
1713 ——— Spengleri
1714 ——— corrugatus, four specimens, two of which have their epidermis
1715 ——— succinctus, several with the epidermis
1716 ——— Pileare
1717 ——— Lotorium
1718 ——— Femorale
1718a ——— Femorale, var. notabilis, latissima, aperturâ expansâ
1719 ——— Pyrum; (a) var. splendida, labio interno varicibusque nigro-maculatis
1720 ——— cynocephalus
1721 ——— Tripus
1722 ——— canaliferus
1723 ——— retusus
1724 ——— Clavator
1725 ——— tuberosus; (a) var. fusca, cingulo prope anfractûs basim albido
1726 ——— chlorostoma
1727 ——— Anus
1728 ——— clathratus
1729 ——— cancellatus
1730 ——— maculosus
1731 ——— clandestinus
1732 ——— Rubecula
1733 ——— cutaceus
1734 ——— doliarius
1735 ——— undosus
1736 ——— affinis, Gmel.
1737 ——— var. T. succincti, testâ albidâ, cingulis elevatis, fuscis

1738 Triton maculosus var. an potiùs species distincta, T. maculoso affinis?
1739 ————
1740 ————
1741 ————
1742 ————

ROSTELLARIA.

1744 Rostellaria curvirostris
1745 ————— rectirostris
1746 ————— Pes Pelecani
1747 ————— an varietas ejusdem? an potiùs
species distincta?

PTEROCERAS.

1748 Pteroceras truncatum
1749 ————— Lambis; *(a)* var. digitis senis
1750 ————— elongatum, Pterocera elongata,
Swains.
1751 ————— Millepeda
1752 ————— Scorpio
1753 ————— aurantiacum, Pt. Aurantia, *Lam.*
1754 ————— purpuratum, Pterocera purpurata,
Swains.
1755 ————— Chiragra, and var.
1756 ————— an testa junior, Pt. truncati var.?

STROMBUS.

1757 Strombus Gigas
1758 ——— accipitrinus
1759 ——— latissimus
1760 ——— tricornis
1761 ——— Gallus; *(a)* var. spirâ brevi
1762 ——— bituberculatus, *St. lobatus, Swains.*
1763 ——— cristatus
1764 ——— bubonius

1763aStrombus lentiginosus
1764a——— Auris-Dianæ; *(b)* var. absque striis transversis
1765 ——— Pacificus, Swains.; *(a)* labio externo supernè cristatim inciso
1766 ——— melanostomus, *S. Melastomus, Swains,* in Bligh Catalogue
1767 ——— Pugilis; *(a)* Strombus Sloanii, *Leach.*
1768 ——— pyrulatus; *(a)* var. albicans
1769 ——— gibberulus
1770 ——— Luhuanus
1771 ——— Mauritianus, *S. cylindricus, Swains.*
1772 ——— Canarium
1773 ——— Isabella
1774 ——— vittatus
1775 ——— Epidromis
1776 ——— Taukervillii, Swains.
1777 ——— succinctus
1778 ——— Troglodytes, St. minimus, Swains.
1779 ——— tridentatus
1780 ——— plicatus
1781 ——— Urceus, varieties; *(a)* an species distincta?
1782 ——— floridus, *St. mutabilis, Swains. (a)* var. minima
1783 ——— Papilio, *Str. exustus. Swains.*
1784 ——— lineatus
1785 ——— marginatus; *(a)* var. testâ transversè sulcatâ
1786 ——— granulatus, *Swains.*
1787 ——— variabilis, *Swains.*
1788 ——— Columba?
1789 ——— galeatus, Swains.
1790 ——— an Str. Goliath? Chemn. xi.
1791 ——— *rugosus*
1792 ——— *gracilior*

1793 Strombus, an St. vittati varietas ? an potiùs species distincta ?

1794 ————— an gracilior St. Urcei varietas, aperturâ angustâ ?

CASSIDARIA.

1795 Cassidaria echinophora
1796 ————— Tyrrhena
1797 ————— Oniscus, Oniscia Oniscus, Sowerby
1798 ————— tuberculosa, Oniscia tuberculosa,
Sowerby

CASSIS.

1799 Cassis Madagascariensis
1800 ——— cornuta
1801 ——— tuberosa
1802 ——— flammea
1803 ——— fasciata
1804 ——— glauca; (a) var. columellâ basi lævi
1805 ——— plicaria
1806 ——— Areola
1807 ——— Zebra
1808 ——— decussata, two varieties
1809 ——— Crumena ?
1810 ——— abbreviata
1811 ——— rufa
1812 ——— pennata
1813 ——— Testiculus; (a) varietas oblonga, spirâ
depressâ
1814 ——— achatina
1815 ——— Zeylanica
1816 ——— sulcosa; (a) var. minor, spirâ productâ;
(b) var. labio incrassato maximo, basi columellæ lævi; (c) var. testâ lævigatâ
1817 ——— granulosa
1818 ——— Saburon
1819 ——— canaliculata

1820 Cassis semigranosa
1821 —————— Vibex
1822 —————— Erinaceus
1823 —————— *coronulata*
1824 —————— ringens, Swainson, in Bligh Catalogue.
     (see Appendix)
1824a—————— Pomum, Dolium Pomum, Lam.
1825 —————— corrugata, Id.
1826 —————— *coarctata*

RICINULA.

1827 Ricinula horrida
1828 —————— clathrata
1829 —————— arachnoidea
1830 —————— digitata; *(a)* var. fusca
1831 —————— Morus
1832 ——————
1833 ——————
1834 ——————
1835 ——————
1836 ——————
1837 ——————
1838 ——————
1839 ——————

PURPURA.

1840 Purpura Persica
1841 —————— Rudolphi
1842 —————— patula
1843 —————— columellaris
1844 —————— succinta; *(a)* var. rugis costiformi-
     bus paucis, latis, asperis
1844a—————— textilosa
1845 —————— Consul
1846 —————— hæmastoma, Buccinum hæmastoma,
     Chemn. xi.
1847 —————— armigera

1848 Purpura bitubercularis
1849 ———— Hippocastanum
1850 ———— undata
1851 ———— hæmastoma? Lam. *query if P. Bufo.*
     several varieties
1852 ———— Mancinella
1853 ———— callosa
1854 ———— neritoides
1855 ———— planospira
1856 ———— callifera
1857 ———— coronata
1858 ———— carinifera
1859 ———— Sacellum
1860 ———— squamosa
1861 ———— rugosa
1862 ———— Sertum
1863 ———— Francolinus
1864 ———— bicostalis
1865 ———— Lapillus
1866 ———— imbricata?
1867 ———— Catarrhacta
1868 ———— echinulata.
1869 ———— Hystrix
1870 ———— Trochlea
1871 ———— Vexillum
1872 ————
1873 ————
1874 ———— an varietas P. bitubercularis?
1875 ————
1876 ————
1877 ————
1878 ————
1879 ————
1880 ————
1881 ———— insignita, Bucc. insignitum, Sol.
1882 ————
1883 ————

MONOCEROS.

Monoceros imbricatum
——————— imbricatum, varietas spirâ brevissimâ ·
——————— glabratum
——————— crassilabrum
——————— cymatum, Bucc. cymatum, Solan.

CONCHOLEPAS.

Concholepas Peruviana.   Of this shell their is
one remarkably fine specimen partly covered
with Balani

HARPA.

Harpa imperialis
——— ventricosa
——— conoidalis
——— nobilis
——— articularis
——— rosea
——— crenata, Swains. in Bligh Catalogue
——— minor
——— cancellata, Chemn. x. t. 152, f. 1453
——— antiqua, Bucc. Harpa antiqua, Chemn.
x. t. 152, f. 1454
——— an varietas H. roseæ?

DOLIUM.

Dolium Galea; *(a)* varietas costis confertis;
(b) spirâ prominente; *(c)* costis interstitiali-
bus duplicatis et triplicatis; *(d)* costis inter-
stitialibus omnibus minoribus, castaneis; aperturâ intus castaneâ, labeo columellari expanso-
castaneo-nigricante
——— Olearium; *(a)* var. sulcis validioribus,
maculis albidis, fuscisque variegata

1903 Dolium maculatum
1904 ———— fasciatum
1905 ———— variegatum
1906 ———— Perdix
1907 ———— an varietas D. maculati? an species distincta?
1908 ———— an varietas D. maculati, costis immaculatis?

BUCCINUM.

1909 Buccinum undatum
1910 ———— glaciale, see Chemn. x. 152, f. 1446-7
1911 ———— Anglicanum
1912 ———— papyraceum
1913 ———— annulatum
1914 ———— lævissimum
1915 ———— testidineum
1916 ———— achatinum
1917 ———— Glans
1918 ———— papillosum
1920 ———— olivaceum
1921 ———— canaliculatum
1922 ———— reticulatum
1923 ———— Tranquebaricum
1924 ———— lineolatum
1925 ———— maculosum
1926 ———— politum
1927 ———— suturale
1928 ———— mutabile
1929 ———— inflatum
1930 ———— gemmulatum
1931 ———— Miga
1932 ———— Ascanias?
1933 ———— Arcularia; (a) var. b. Lam.
1934 ———— coronatum
1935 ———— Thersites; (a) var. minor
1936 ———— gibbosulum

1937 Buccinum Pullus?

1938 ———— neriteum, three varieties, or perhaps distinct species

1939 ———— plumbeum, Chemn. xɪ. t. 188, f. 1806, 1807

1940 ———— Lima, Chemn. xɪ. t. 188, f. 1808, 1809

1941 ———— lineatum, Murex lineatus, Chemn. x. t. 164, f. 1572

1942 ———— varicosum, ——— varicosus Chemn. x. t. 162, f. 1546, 1547

1943 ———— turgidum, Dillw.

1944 ———— Australe, Chemn. x. t. 154, f. 1477

1945 ———— cassideum, Chemn. x. t. 153, f. 1463, 1464

1946 ——— Cochlidium? Dillw. and Chemn.

1947 ————

1948 ————

1949 ————

1950 ———— Humphreysianum, Bennet in Zool. Journ. vol. ɪ.

1951 ————

1952 ————

1953 ————

1954 ————

1955 ————

1956 ————

1957 ————

1958 ———— *melanostoma*

EBURNA.

Obs. While we gladly adopt the improvement, suggested by ourselves and established by Mr. Swainson, of separating Lamarck's *Eburna glabrata* from the other shells included by Lamarck in his genus Eburna and placing it with *Ancilla*, to which it naturally belongs; we regret that we cannot approve his reasons for continuing the generic name *Eburna* to the shells which he proposes to leave in the present genus, principally because it will be remembered that the typical species of the genus, and the only one to which the name could be properly applied, which species is commonly called " *L'Ivoire*" in French, is that which Mr. S. separates from it, actually taking away the species to which the name was originally applied and leaving those to which it is not applicable. Should it not be thought advisable to restore these to *Buccinum*, it appears to us proper to alter the name: because we think it better to give a name without any signification than to convey an erroneous idea.

1959 Eburna Zeylanica
1960 ——— spirata
1961 ——— areolata
1962 ——— Valentiana, Swains.
1963 ——— *papillaris*
1964 ——— *Ambulacrum*

TEREBRA.

1965 Terebra maculata
1966 ——— flammea
1967 ——— crenulata
1968 ——— dimidiata
1969 ——— muscaria
1970 ——— subulata
1971 ——— oculata
1972 ——— duplicata
1973 ——— striatula
1974 ——— Myuros
1975 ——— scabrella
1976 ——— strigilata
1977 ——— leanceata

1978 Terebra aciculina
1979 ———— cærulescens; *(a)* var. major, albida, superne maculis fuscis picta.
1980 ———— vittata
1981 ———— hastata, Bucc. hastatum, Dillw.
1982 ———— felina, ——— felinum, Dillw.
1983 ———— *lineolata*
1984 ———— *strigata*
1985 ———— *fusco-maculata*
1986 ———— *punctulata*
1987 ———— *tricolor*
1988 ———— pertusa? Dillw.
1989 ———— *nebeculata*
1990 ———— *nebulosa*
1991 ———— an varietas T. fusco-maculatæ?
1992 ———— ————— " The clouded and chequered Needle," Budgin MS.
1993 ———— an varietas T. Myuri?
1994 ————
1995 ————
1996 ————
1997 ————
1998 ————
1999 ————
2000 ————
2001 ————

COLUMBELLA.

2002 Columbella strombiformis
2003 ———— rustica
2004 ———— mercatoria
2005 ———— semipunctata
2006 ———— bizonalis; an proprie ad Mitras referenda?
2007 ———— reticulata
2008 ———— ovulata
2009 ———— fulgurans

2010 Columbella mendicaria
2011 ———————— punctata
2012 ———————— concinna, Sowerbys' Genera
2013 ———————— Terpsichore, Id.
2014 ———————— *fasciata*, Voluta fasciata, Budg. MS.
2015 ————————
2016 ————————
2017 ————————
2018 ————————
2019 ———————— guttata, Bucc. guttatum, Soland.
2020 ————————
2021 ————————
2022 ————————
2023 ————————

MITRA.

2024 Mitra episcopalis
2025 ——— papalis
2026 ——— pontificalis
2027 ——— Millepora
2028 ——— Diadema, Swains. in Bligh Catalogue
2029 ——— Cardinalis
2030 ——— nivosa, Swains. Exot. Conch.
2031 ——— terebralis
2032 ——— adusta
2033 ——— granulosa
2034 ——— crocata
2035 ——— casta
2036 ——— olivaria
2037 ——— granatina
2038 ——— scabriuscula
2039 ——— crenifera
2040 ——— serpentina
2041 ——— tæniata
2942 ——— Regina, *Swains.*
2043 ——— plicaria
2044 ——— corrugata

2045 Mitra costellaris
2046 ——— lyrata
2047 ——— Melongena
2048 ——— Vulpecula
2049 ——— Caffra, *M. bifasciata*, Swains.
2050 ——— Sanguisuga. This and the following are undoubtedly variations of the same species, only different in the arrangement of their colours
2051 ——— stigmataria
2052 ——— filosa, three distinct varieties
2053 ——— lectea
2054 ——— cornicularis
2055 ——— striatula?
2056 ——— Tringa?
2057 ——— melaniana, an Mitra carbonaria, Sw.?
2058 ——— scutulata
2059 ——— Dactylus
2060 ——— crenulata
2061 ——— texturata
2062 ——— limbifera
2063 ——— aurantiaca
2064 ——— paupercula
2064*a*——— retusa, Voluta Vacca, Sol.
2065 ——— cucumerina
2066 ——— torulosa? several varieties
2067 ——— Ebenus
2068 ——— semifasciata?
2069 ——— microzonia
2070 ——— demestina
2071 ——— pertusa var. Swains. Zool. Ill.
2072 ——— rigida, Swains. Zool. Ill.
2073 ——— vittata, Swains. Zool. Ill.
2074 ——— contracta, Swains. Zool. Ill.
2075 ——— scabricula, Chemn. xi. t. 179, f. 1729-30
2076 ——— granosa, Chemn. x. t. 151, f. 1442-3
2077 ——— cruentata, Chemn. x. t. 151, f. 1438-9
2078 ——— subdivisa, Chemn. x. t. 151, f. 1434-5

2079 Mitra ead. var. Chemn. x. t. 151, f. 1436-7
2080 ———— cancellata? Swains. Zool. Ill.
2081 ————
2082 ————
2083 ————
2084 ———— porcata, *Vol. porcata, Sol.*
2085 ————
2086 ————
2087 ————
2088 ———— inops, *Voluta Inops. Sol.*
2089 ———— matronalis, *Voluta matronalis, Sol.*
2090 ————
2091 ————
2092 ————
2093 ————
2094 ———— *succincta,* Swains. see Appendix
2095 ———— *sulcata,* Id.
2096 ———— *leucostoma,* Id.
2097 ———— *rugosa,* Id.
2098 ———— an M. tæniatæ var.? Id.
2099 ———— ———— remarkable for its resemblance
to an *Oliva.*

CONOHELIX, *Swains.*

2100 Conohelix marmorata, Swains. Zool. Ill.
2101 ———— lineata, Swains. Zool. Ill.

VOLUTA.

2102 ———— Voluta nautica
2103 ———— Diadema
2104 ———— armata
2105 ———— ducalis, two varieties
2106 ———— Æthiopica
2107 ———— Melo, in several stages of growth and
varieties
2108 ———— Neptuni
2109 ———— Cymbium

Voluta Olla; *(a)* monstrosa

—— proboscidalis

—— porcina

—— Scapha

—— Brasiliana

—— an testæ juniores Volutæ Neptuni?

—— testæ juniores, Vol. Cymbii

—— imperialis

—— Pellis-Serpentis

—— Vespertilio? *(a)* tuberculis obtusis; colore carneo, rubro-variegato

—— mitis

—— nivosa

—— serpentina

—— Hebræa

—— Musica; *(a)* monstrosa

—— Thiarella

—— polyzonalis

—— Guinaica

—— carneolata

—— sulcata

—— magnifica

—— Ancilla

—— Magellanica

—— Pacifica

—— fulminata

—— undulata

—— Lapponica

—— Vexillum; *(a)* tuberculis obsoletis

—— volvacea, *Mart. Conch.* III. t. 95. f. 922-3

—— Nucleus

—— lyrata, *Humphrey's MS.?*

—— angulata, *Swains. Exot. Conch.*

—— marmorata, *Swains. Exot. Conch.*

—— Zebra, *Leach's Misc. Zool.* Marginella radiata, *Lam.*

—— lineata, *Leach's Misc. Zool.; (a)* var. lineis aurantiacis pallidis

2145 Voluta *Cymbiola*, Chemn. x. t. 148, f. 1385, 1386, *Vol. calcarata*, Sol. MS.—*Obs.* This fine shell was originally in the celebrated Portland Cabinet, No. 4036

2146 ————— *pulchra*

2147 ————— fusiformis, Swains. in Bligh Catalogue

2148 ————— papillosa, Swains. in Bligh Catalogue

2149 ————— *fulgetrum*

2150 ————— *Aulica*, Solander.—*Obs.* An extremely scarce and fine shell; the only specimen we have seen

MARGINELLA.

2151 Marginella glabella

2151a ————— *Goodalli*

2152 ————— aurantiaca?

2153 ————— nubeculata

2154 ————— cærulescens, several varieties

2155 ————— quinque-plicata

2156 ————— limbata

2157 ————— bifasciata

2158 ————— Faba

2159 ————— bivaricosa

2160 ————— longivaricosa

2161 ————— bullata.— *Obs.* Lamarck refers to figures of two very distinct shells under this name; the specimens that exist in this collection are the same as Chemnitz's, x. t. 150, f. 1409, 1410, and as the specimen referred to by Swainson in the Bligh Catalogue.

2162 ————— Persicula

2163 ————— lineata

2164 ————— interrupta?

2165 ————— undulata, *Voluta glabella undulata*, Chemn. x. t. 150, f. 1423, 1424. *V. Strigata*, *Dillw.*

2166 ————— marginata, *Vol. marginata*, *Chemn.* x. t. 150, f. 1421

2167 Marginella guttata, *Sol. MS. Dillw.*
2168 ———————— picta, *Dillw.*
2169 ———————— catenata, *Vol. catenata, Montagu.*
2170 ———————— Monilis, *Voluta Monilis,* Dillw. *Vol-*
.   *varia Monilis,* Lam.
2171 ————————
2172 ————————
2173 ———————— Chemnitzii, Voluta, Dillw.
2174 ————————
2175 ————————
2176 ————————
2177 ————————
2178 ————————
2179 ———————— pallida, *Volvaria pallida,* Lam.
2180 ———————— triticea, *Volvaria tritica,* Lam.
2181 ————————
2182 ————————
2182a ———————— miliaria

OVULA.

2183 Ovula oviformis
2184 ———— angulosa
2185 ———— verrucosa
2186 ———— carnea
2187 ———— gibbosa
2188 ———— acicularis
2189 ———— Spelta
2190 ———— birostris
2191 ———— Volva

CYPRÆA.

Obs. The Cyprææ are named according to Gray's
article on Cypræideæ in Zoological Journal,
vol. i.

2192 Cypræa Mappa, several fine varieties
2193 ———— Arabica, numerous specimens and varieties

2194 Cypræa Mauritiana
2195 ———— stercoraria
2196 ———— Scurra
2197 ———— testudinaria
2198 ———— Exanthema and cervina
2199 ———— Argus
2200 ———— Talpa
2201 ———— Isabella
2202 ———— lurida
2203 ———— cinerea
2204 ———— carneola
2205 ———— arenosa
2206 ———— sulcidentata
2207 ———— achatina
2208 ———— Aurora
2209 ———— tessellata
2210 ———— Vittellus
2211 ———— Lynx
2212 ———— Tigris
2213 ———— pantherina
2214 ———— Onyx
2215 ———— Pyrum
2216 ———— undata
2217 ———— Zigzag
2218 ———— clandestina; *(a)* var. cingulo transver-
    so, elevato
2219 ———— Asellus
2220 ———— interrupta
2221 ———— Hirundo
2222 ———— stolida, *C. rubiginosa* vulgò
2223 ———— punctata
2224 ———— tebescens?
2225 ———— cylindrica
2226 ———— cribraria
2227 ———— fimbriata
2228 ———— felina
2229 ———— erronea
2230 ———— zonata

2231 Cypræa sanguinolenta
2232 ———— cruenta
2233 ———— Caurica
2234 ———— Moneta
2235 ———— obvelata
2236 ———— Annulus
2237 ———— Caput-Serpentis
2238 ———— Mus
2239 ———— angustata
2240 ———— spadicea
2241 ———— Turdus
2242 ———— spurca
2243 ———— gangrenosa
2244 ———— erosa
2245 ———— an varietas C. erosæ? an species dis-
    tincta? testâ subtus albidâ, fusco-purpureo
    lineatâ et punctatâ
2246 ———— ocellata
2247 ———— Lamarckii
2248 ———— Listeri
2249 ———— Helvola
2250 ———— poraria
2251 ———— albuginosa
2252 ———— staphylæa, numerous specimens and
    varieties
2253 ———— pustulata
2254 ———— Madagascariensis
2255 ———— Nucleus
2256 ———— Cicerula
2257 ———— Globulus
2258 ———— Childreni
2259 ———— lentiginosa, *C. sabulosa, Sol. MS.*
2260 ———— *umbilicata,* Nobis, see Appendix
2261 ———— *melanostoma,* Leathes MS. see Appendix
2262 ———— aperta, Swainson, in Bligh Catalogue.
    Obs. This shell accords perfectly with La-
    marck's description of C. Oniscus, but it does
    not agree with the figure of Martini which he
    cites.

2263 Cypræa radians, Lam.
2264 ———— Pediculus, Lam.
2265 ———— Oryza, Lam. nivea, Leathes MS.
2266 ———— ovulata, Lam.
2267 ———— Europea, Mont.
2268 ———— Margarita, Dillw.
2269 ———— exilis, *Gmel.*
2270 ————
2271 ————
2272 ———— pellucida, Leathes MS.
2273 ———— conspurcata, Id.
2274 ———— Pulex
2275 ————
2276 ———— rosea
2277 ————
2278 ————

TEREBELLUM.

2279 Terebellum subulatum

ANCILLARIA.

2280 Ancillaria candida, Swains. in Journ. of Sci-
     ence, Lit. and Arts, No. 36.
2281 ———— cinnamomea, Id.
2282 ———— fulva, Id.
2283 ———— ventricosa, Id.
2284 ———— marginata, Id. var. immaculata
2285 ———— Tankervillii, Id.—*Obs.* Without en-
     tering into a particular description of this
     shell, we shall merely remark that there is a
     small tooth near the base of the outer lip; and
     that near the base of the body volution, and
     between it and the inner lip, are to be ob-
     served two grooves, of which the upper one
     is much the deeper, corresponding to the
     grooves formed by the lower part of the um-
     bilicus in A. glabrata. Three specimens of

this shell were in Mr. G. Humphrey's collection.

2286 Ancillaria balteata, Id.
2287 ——— glabrata, Id.
2288 ——— *aperta*
2289 ——— albifasciata?—*Obs.* This shell does not accord well with Swainson's description of A. albifasciata; we have not, however, ventured to describe it as distinct, because we have no authentic specimen of his A. albifasciata to compare it with.

OLIVA.

2290 Oliva porphyria
2291 ——— textilina
2292 ——— erythrostoma
2293 ——— Pica
2294 ——— tremulina
2295 ——— angulata
2296 ——— Maura
2297 ——— Sepulturalis
2298 ——— fulminans
2299 ——— elegans
2300 ——— episcopalis
2301 ——— venulata?
2302 ——— guttata; (*a*) var. alba
2303 ——— reticularis
2304 ——— flammulata
2305 ——— araneosa
2306 ——— litterata
2307 ——— tricolor
2308 ——— sanguinolenta
2308*a* ——— mustelina
2308*b* ——— lugubris
2309 ——— funebralis?
2310 ——— Senegalensis
2311 ——— fusiformis

2312a Oliva undata
2312b ——— inflata
2312c ——— bicincta
2313 ——— harpularia
2314 ——— ustulata
2315 ——— tessellata
2316 ——— carneola
2317 ——— ispidula
2318 ——— candida
2319 ——— tigrina
2320 ——— Brasiliana
2321 ——— utriculus
2322 ——— auricularia
2323 ——— acuminata
2324 ——— subulata?
2325 ——— hiatula; (a) var. alba
2326 ——— conoidalis
2327 ——— eburnea
2328 ——— nana
2329 ——— Oryza
2330 ——— *splendidula*
2331 ——— *patula*, Voluta patula, Sol. MS.
2331a ——— ——— var.
2332 ——— *biplicata*
2333 ——— *columellaris*
2334 ——— var. monstrosa, labio externo reflexo
2335 ——— var. O. Mauræ, monstrosa, anfractibus supernè angulato-depressis, ambulacrum planum spirale efformante
2336 ——— var. monstrosa, sulco suturali maximo, marginibus subinflexis
2337 ——— var. O. ispidulæ, testâ subfuscâ, cingulo elevato, centrali, pallidiore. From Ceylon.

CONUS.

2338 Conus marmoreus
2339 ——— Bandanus
2340 ——— nocturnus

Conus Nicobaricus
———— araneosus
———— zonatus, several fine varieties
———— imperialis
———— fuscatus
———— viridulus
———— regius, two remarkably fine specimens
———— Cedo-nulli
———— aurantiacus
———— nebulosus
———— minimus, two varieties
———— sulcatus
———— Hebræus
———— vermiculatus; *(a)* var. testâ longitudinaliter costatâ, costis granosis
———— arenatus; *(a)* var. [b] **Lam.** *punctis
minutissimis, spirâ acutâ; (b)* var. [c] **Lam.**
granulosa; (c) specimen with its epidermis
———— pulicarius
———— fustigatus
———— obesus
———— varius
———— Tulipa
———— Geographus; *(a)* specimen with its
epidermis
———— punctatus
———— tæniatus
———— Ceylanensis
———— miliaris
———— Mus
———— lividus
———— Cardinalis
———— Magellanicus var.
———— distans
———— sponsalis
———— pusillus
———— asper

2374 Conus millepunctatus
2375 ———— litteratus
2376 ———— eberneus
2377 ———— tessellatus
2378 ———— Generalis, many varieties
2379 ———— Maldivus
2380 ———— Malaccanus
2381 ———— lineatus
2382 ———— Monile
2383 ———— Centurio
2384 ———— vitulinus
2385 ———— vulpinus
2386 ———— flavidus
2387 ———— Virgo
2388 ———— Daucus
2389 ———— Pastinaca
2390 ———— Capitaneus
2391 ———— Classiarius
2392 ———— mustelinus
2393 ———— Vexillum
2394 ———— Sumatrensis
2395 ———— Miles
2396 ———— Ammiralis.—*Obs.* It is needless to enu-
       merate the varieties of this beautiful shell;
       it is sufficient to state that the series consists
       of several specimens of extraordinary size
       and brilliancy, together with three specimens
       of the granulated variety.
2397 ———— Genuanus
2398 ———— papilionaceus
2399 ———— Siamensis
2400 ———— Prometheus
2401 ———— glaucus
2402 ———— Suratensis
2403 ———— Monachus
2404 ———— Achatinus
2405 ———— cinereus
2406 ———— stramineus

M

2407 Conus Mercator
2408 ——— ochraceus
2409 ——— betulinus
2410 ——— figulinus, and varieties
2411 ——— quercinus
2412 ——— Proteus
2413 ——— leoninus
2414 ——— Augur
2415 ——— fulgurans
2416 ——— acuminatus; *(a)* monstrum
2417 ——— Amadis
2418 ——— Janus
2419 ——— Lithoglyphus
2420 ——— testudinarius
2421 ——— Quæstor? C. characteristicus, Chemn.
2422 ——— Mozambicus
2423 ——— guinaicus
2424 ——— Franciscanus
2425 ——— Rattus
2426 ——— Catus
2427 ——— puncticulatus
2428 ——— Mindanus
2429 ——— Columba
2430 ——— Tinianus
2431 ——— amabilis
2432 ——— Omaïcus
2433 ——— nobilis
2434 ——— nobilis var. b.
2435 ——— Aurisiacus
2436 ——— striatus
2437 ——— Gubernator
2438 ——— granulatus
2439 ——— Terebra
2440 ——— Raphanus
2441 ——— Magus
2442 ——— Spectrum; *(a)* var. fulvo nebulosa
2443 ——— bullatus
2444 ——— Curvus, testæ juniores

2445 Conus Stercus muscarum

2446 ———— Timorensis ? *C. vespertinus*, tab. nost.—
Obs. This shell accords perfectly well with
Lamarck's description of Conus Timorensis,
but the figure to which he refers is far from
exhibiting the elegant form of our shell, probably on account of its having been drawn
from a bad specimen. This cone is named
" vespertinus, the Sun-set," on a ticket in
George Humphrey's hand-writing in the collection.

2447 ———— nimbosus

2448 ———— Dux

2449 ———— tendineus

2450 ———— Glans

2451 ———— Nussatella

2452 ———— Aulicus

2453 ———— Auratus

2454 ———— Clavus

2455 ———— auricomus

2456 ———— Omaria

2457 ———— rubiginosus

2458 ———— pennaceus

2459 ———— Archiepiscopus

2460 ———— Abbas

2461 ———— Legatus

2462 ———— Textile, numerous varieties

2463 ———— Gloria-Maris

2464 ———— Australis

2465 ———— Mediterraneus

2466 ————

2467 ————

2468 ————

2469 ————

2470 ———————————— Encycl. Meth. t. 343, f. 5

2471 ————

2472 ————

2473 ————

1 Conus
5 ————
5 ————
7 ————
3 ————
9 ————

SPIRULA.

9 Spirula Peronii

NAUTILUS.

1 Nautilus Pompilius
2 ———— umbilicatus
3 ———— scrobiculatus

ARGONAUTA.

1 Argonauta Argo
5 ———— tuberculosus
3 ———— nitidus
7 ————

APPENDIX.

22. SERPULA FUSCATA.

S. testâ irregulariter contortâ; lineis elevatis, interruptis, obsoletiusculis; colore violaceo-fusco.

Obs. A specimen of this shell is named Serpula
fuscata in Mr. Geo. Humphrey's collection. The
tube is very large, being more than an inch wide in
some parts.

23. SERPULA MAXIMA.

S. testâ irregulariter contortâ, læviusculâ, carinâ dorsali antice in spinam nonnunquam desinente: aperturâ expansâ, testarum juniorum subtrigonâ, operculo corneo.

Obs. Several specimens of this species exist in
the collection; they are attached to, and some of
them deeply imbedded in coral. It is a very large
species, the tubes being almost an inch wide. The
aperture in the older shells is round.

24. SERPULA TRICUSPIDATA.

S. testâ elongatâ, tenui, trigonâ, basi affixâ, demum
porrectâ; carinâ dorsali primùm denticulatâ; aperturâ tricuspidatâ.

Obs. Two specimens of Terebratula vitrea in
this collection are adorned with several of this singular species of Serpula, which does not appear to
be noticed either by Lamarck or Dillwyn, although
it has been long known to collectors.

58. ASPERGILLUM SPARSUM.

A. vaginâ lævi, disco postico fimbriâ radiatâ circumdato, tubulis fimbriæ majusculis, poris disci postici
majusculis, sparsis.

Obs. It is rather doubtful which of the two species in this collection (leaving A. vaginiferum out of
the question) ought to be considered as A. Javanum
and which is undescribed by Lamarck. The great
differences consist in the number and size of the
tubes of which the radiated fringe is composed, and
in the number and size of the perforations in the
disk, both of which, in the species I have here called
A. sparsum, are twice as large and not half so numerous as in that which I have considered as A. Javanum.

116. MACTRA ELEGANS.

M. testâ rotundato-trigonâ, tumidâ, tenui, anticè
acutè carinatâ, superficie eleganter concentricè
sulcatâ; sulcis rotundatis.

Obs. A much rounder and more tumid shell than
Mactra plicataria.

117. MACTRA ASPERSA.

M. testâ ellipticâ, inæquilaterali, antico latere postico
dupló longiore, umbonibus subprominentibus, superficie sulcis transversis obsoletiusculis; colore
albido, fusco asperso.

Obs. This shell resembles Venus virginea in
general form, like that shell it is smooth and slightly
grooved transversely; it is, however, of a whitish
colour speckled with brown.

121. CRASSATELLA RADIATA.

C. testâ arcuatâ, anticè acutè rostratâ, carinatâ; superficie arcuato-sulcatâ, maculis spadiceis interruptis radiatâ.

Obs. An interesting and beautiful small shell, with whose locality we are not acquainted; it is, however, probably from New Holland.

150. PSAMMOTÆA CARNEA.

P. testâ ovali, subgibbosâ, carneâ, umbonibus profundioribus.

184. TELLINA PULCHERRIMA.

T. testâ transversim oblongâ, latere altero rotundato, altero acutangulo; pallidâ, roseo radiatâ, disco centrali læviusculo, obliquè striato, extremitatibus squamuloso-asperis: intus pallidè aurantiacâ.

198. TELLINIDES OVALIS.

T. testâ ovali, læviusculâ, subæquilaterali, latere altero rotundato, altero subangulato; roseâ, radiis exiguis albidis.

199. TELLINIDES EMARGINATUS.

T. testâ oblongâ, inæquilaterali, læviusculâ, latere antico breviore, subangulato et emarginato; plicaturâ in utrâque valvâ symmetricâ.

Obs.—The posterior side is rounded and double the length of the anterior: the umbones are pale orange colour, and within there are two darker oblong orange spots passing from the umbo to each muscular impression in each valve. From Brazil.

200. TELLINIDES TRUNCATULUS.

T. testâ oblongâ, inæquilaterali, lævi, latere antico breviore, rotundato-truncato, plicaturâ obsoletiusculâ in utrâque valvâ symmetricâ.

Obs.—In general form this nearly resembles the last, the anterior side is, however, proportionably rather longer: the fold in the anterior side does not form a deep groove as in the last, nor is there an evident notch in the edge: the shell is white and its umbones are pale orange within and without. From the East Indies.

201. TELLINIDES POLITUS.

T. testâ obliquè subtrigonâ, politâ, latere postico breviore, rotundato; antico prominente, lineis excentricis, elevatis, sparsis.

Obs.—Of a pale testaceous colour and with a shining surface: its locality is unknown to us.

226. DONAX TRANSVERSA.

D. testâ transversim elongatâ, lævi; latere postico brevi, biangulato, carinato, obliquè truncato, longitudinaliter sulcato; extus albidâ; fulvo obsoletè radiatâ,

Obs.—This is longer in a transverse direction than any other species we know.

354*b*. VENERICARDIA CRASSICOSTATA.

V. testâ cordatâ, tumidâ, posticè angulatâ; costis 22 crassis, depressis, lateribus angulatis, irregulariter crenatis.

Obs. A single valve, white within, and varied on the outside with pink, orange, crimson, and dark brown

398. CARDITA SQUAMOSUS.

C. testâ oblongâ, costis 16, squamosis, squamis albis.
    Obs. A very pretty little shell, from Pulo Condore

399. CARDITA SQUAMIFERUS.

C. testâ oblongâ, anticè coarctatâ, costis 12 squamiferis; squamis latis.

Obs. Three of the ribs are much larger and broader than the remaining nine, and the posterior part of the shell is rather flattened.

400. CARDITA INCRASSATUS.

C. testâ oblongâ, anticè brevi, costis 16 incrassatis, rotundatis, crenatis; interstitiis angustis.

Obs. There are two specimens of this shell, which do not accord with any of the representations of Cardita sulcatus, though it is commonly known by the name of *Chama antiquata.*

531. PINNA SERRATA.

P. testâ tenui, subpellucidâ, corneâ, costis radiantibus creberrimis, concinnè et minutissimè muricatis, latere altero acutissimo, altero retuso, margine cardinis recto, in utrâque valvâ serrifero.

Obs. A most elegant shell, somewhat resembling P. pectinata in appearance; its most remarkable character is its double row of spines on the hinge margin.

531a. PINNA ATRO-PURPUREA.

P. testâ atro-purpurea, costis radiantibus, muticis, distantibus; margine cardinali longitudinem lateralis æquante latere postico arcuato.

692. CHITON LATUS.

C. testâ latâ, valvis arcuatis, lævibus, creberrimè sulcatis, olivaceis, albido-punctulatis.

Obs. The locality is not known.

693. CHITON RUGULOSUS.

C. testâ, valvarum *parte mediana* longitudinaliter rugulosâ, *laterali* concinnè radiatâ.

794. FISSURELLA APERTA.

F. testâ ovatâ, carneâ, fusco-radiatâ, margine inte-
grâ, albâ, depressâ; foramine ovato, magno : long.
1 unc. lat. $\frac{1}{2}$ unc.

Obs. There are two specimens of this shell,
which is easily distinguished by its large ovate, entire foramen, independently of the depressed white
margin, which is probably caused by the mantle of
the animal overlapping the edge of the shell.

795. FISSURELLA CLYPEIFORMIS.

F. testâ ovato-oblongâ, depressiusculâ, lævi, extus
fuscâ; foramine elongato, intus integro, extus lateribus coarctatis, utrinque unidentatis; margine
undulatâ; infrà albidâ : long. $2\frac{9}{10}$ unc. lat. $1\frac{7}{10}$
unc.

796. FISSURELLA CRENULATA.

F. testâ oblongo-ovatâ, depressâ, albâ; foramine ovato, integro; superficie striis confertis, radiantibus, decussatis; margine crenulatâ; long. $3\frac{4}{10}$ unc.
lat. $2\frac{1}{10}$ unc.

Obs. Besides these three undescribed species
there are the six following, viz. Nos. 797 to 802, which
do not appear to be mentioned by Lamarck, yet we
have not ventured to describe them, on account of
the extreme difficulty of ascertaining whether or not
they are already noticed.

808. SIPHONARIA GIGAS.

S. testâ suborbiculari, conicâ, radiatim carinato-
costatâ, costis distantibus; vertice recto, centrali :
long. $2\frac{5}{10}$ *unc.* lat. 2 *unc.*

Obs. This is the largest species of the genus we
have seen: from Panama.

809. SIPHONARIA OBLIQUATA.

S. testâ oblongâ, extus radiatim obtusè costatâ ; vertice suobliquè et posticè inclinato : long. 1 $\frac{9}{10}$ unc.
lat. 1 $\frac{1}{10}$ unc.

Obs. From Van Diemen's Land ; we had not
seen these two species when we first described the
genus.

821. CALYPTRÆA COMMA-NOTATA.

C. testâ suborbiculari, depresso-conicâ, vertice centrali, maculâ fuscâ, subconvolutâ, a vertice ad mar-
ginem decurrente.

Obs. From the coast of Guinea.

828. CREPIDULA ADUNCA.

C. testâ subovali, vertice adunco, margine undatâ,
labio interno septiformi.

Obs. The internal septiform lip divides the ca-
vity nearly in the middle—the upper being the
smaller portion ; this is very deep.

973. COCHLOGENA MAXIMA.

C. testâ oblongo-ovatâ, spirâ productâ, anfractibus
rotundato-ventricosis, ore albo : long. 6 unc. lat.
3 $\frac{1}{4}$ unc.

Obs. Two specimens of this shell are in the collection. It is principally distinguished from the two
following, viz. 974 and 975, by its size, its ventricose
volutions, and its white lip. Locality unknown.

997. PARTULA UNIDENTATA.

P. testâ oblongo-ovatâ, anfractibus 4 ad 5, rotundatis ; aperturâ castaneâ, labio externo internè uni-
dentato, dente valido, obtuso.

Obs. About two inches long and one broad, of a pale rose colour; edge of the aperture chesnut. Locality unknown.

1015. CYCLOSTOMA FIMBRIATULUM.

C. testâ obtusè conicâ, umbilicatâ, acfractibus 4, ventricosis, transversim sulcatis, creberrimè decussatis, suturis profundis; labii margine plicato-fimbriato: long. $\frac{5}{10}$ unc. lat. $\frac{6}{10}$ unc.

Obs. A very pretty little shell, bearing a considerable resemblance to No. 1014.   From Jamaica.

1016. CYCLOSTOMA UNIFASCIATUM.

C. testâ ovato-conoideâ, apice truncatâ, lævi, umbilicatâ, anfractibus rotundatis; labio extus marginato: colore albido, fasciâ anfractuum fuscâ, unicâ. Long. $\frac{4}{10}$ unc. lat. $\frac{5}{10}$ unc.

Obs. From Guinea.

1024. HELICINA LENTICULARIS.

H. testâ globoso-lenticulari, carinatâ, lævi, supernè aurantiacâ, suturâ albâ; aperturâ extus angulatâ: subtus pallidâ, convexiusculâ; peristomate incrassato; columellâ basi callosâ, aurantiacâ.

Obs. This little shell approaches very near to H. viridis, *Gray*, in general form, but is easily distinguished.   From the South Sea Islands: one specimen.

1036. LIMNÆA TIMORENSIS.

L. testâ sinistrorsâ, oblongâ, spirâ acuminatâ, lævi, tenuiter striatâ, anfractibus quinque rotundatis, ultimo majusculo: aperturâ oblongâ, labio interno minimè expanso. Long. $\frac{8}{10}$ unc. lat. $\frac{9}{10}$ unc.

Obs. From Timor.

1039. LIMNÆA SUBGLOBOSA.

L. testâ ovato-subglobosâ, spirâ brevissimâ, acutiusculâ; anfractu ultimo ventricoso; aperturâ amplâ.
Long. $\frac{7}{10}$ unc. lat. $\frac{5}{10}$ unc.

Obs. This is the roundest species of Limnæa I
have seen, it is of a dirty black colour, the lips very
thin, hornlike, and of a pale colour. Locality unknown.

1048a. MELANIA INERMIS.

M. testâ obovatâ, lævi, fuscâ, anfractibus 3 ad 4, ventricosis, suturâ validâ; aperturâ lacteâ, margine
nigro: long. 1 unc. lat. $\frac{7}{10}$ unc.

Obs. If the characters of the aperture were not
carefully observed, this shell would be ranked with
the Paludinæ. Both the specimens in this collection
are eroded at the apices. From Georgia. *Helix im-
perfecta,* Budgen MS. We have named it *inermis,*
because, though nearly resembling M. Amarula in
general appearance, it is destitute of spines.

1056. MELANOPSIS LABIATA.

M. testâ ellipticâ, tuberculato-tricarinatâ, spirâ
brevi, acuminatâ, aperturâ ovatâ; labio columellari incrassato, expanso, infra calloso: intus albâ,
castaneo-trifasciatâ. Long $\frac{5}{10}$ unc. lat. $\frac{7}{10}$ unc.

*Obs. Buccinum olivaceum, Solander MS. The
small knotted greenish Buccinum, Budgin MS.*

1069. PALUDINA OLIVACEA.

P. testâ sinistrorsâ, oblongâ, lævi, olivaceâ, anfractibus 5 ad 6, ultimo maximo; umbilico parvo;
aperturâ ovatâ, supernè acutâ: long. $2\frac{1}{10}$ unc. lat.
$1\frac{5}{10}$ unc.

Obs. This is the only specimen of this fine shell
we have ever seen. We have rather doubted whe-

o

ther it should be placed here or in **Ampullaria**, nevertheless in those few particulars in which the Paludinæ differ from the Ampullariæ, this shell accords more nearly with the Paludinæ. Locality unknown.

1070. PALUDINA BICOLOR.

P. testâ oblongo-conicâ, apice obtuso, anfractibus subquinis, convexiusculis, olivaceis, strigis quatuor vel quinque transversis, elevatis, fuscis ornatâ : long. $\frac{17}{10}$ unc. lat. $\frac{11}{10}$ unc.

Obs. From Canton. I have long known this shell, but do not find it described anywhere.

1089. AMPULLARIA MEGASTOMA.

A. testâ subglobosâ, longitudinaliter undulato-striatâ ; spirâ brevissimâ, depressâ ; anfractu ultimo maximo, superne rotundato-angulato ; umbilico minimo, juxta labii columellaris medium posito ; aperturâ amplissimâ, supernè subangulatâ, infra rotundatâ : latitudine longitudinem fere æquante.

Obs. The only specimen of this singular shell that we have seen; it is about three inches long, the same in breadth, and of a pale colour, with transverse fuscous bands; the inside is irregularly coloured with a brownish violaceous tinge. Locality unknown.

1092. NAVICELLA SUBORBICULARIS.

N. testâ suborbiculari, cavitate profundiore, vertice submarginali.

Obs. This species nearly resembles N. elliptica : its greater diameter is to its smaller as 5 to 4 : its vertex is not quite marginal : it is white, with an orange spot within the vertex, and it is externally marked with triangular white spots, whose interstices are finely reticulated with a dark violet colour. Epidermis of a light olivaceous brown. From Timor.

1094. NERITINA CANALIS.

N. testâ ovatâ, spirâ brevissimâ, obtectâ, labio externo in canalem ad sinistram inclinatam producto, labio columellari aurantiaco, obsoletè subdenticulato; epidermide nigerrimâ. Long. $\frac{1}{10}$, lat. 1 unc.

Obs. This shell very nearly resembles N. pulligera, we think, however, that it will be distinguished by the characters given above; its epidermis is very black, and its inner lip of a fine orange colour. All the specimens in this collection are rather smaller than the full grown N. pulligeræ. From the Islands of the South Seas.

1115. NERITINA GRANOSA.

N. testâ subrotundâ, compressiusculâ, subalatâ, albâ, epidermide nigrâ indutâ, extus granosâ, granis per series ordinatis; labii externi margine crenulato; subtus planulatâ, labio columellari lato, aurantiaco, margine interno sinuato, edentulo.

Obs. This singular "black tuberculated Nerite" is marked by Mr. Budgin "from a fresh-water stream in one of the South Sea Islands." There are several specimens in the collection, all of which have been pierced near the vertex, from which circumstance it is supposed that they have served as ornaments.

1170. NATICA VIOLACEA.

N. testâ conoideo-subglobulosâ, albâ, castaneo maculatâ et strigatâ; maculis per series quinque ordinatis; spirâ acutiusculâ, umbilico fere obtecto,

callo columellari roseo, operculo testaceo : long.
$\frac{8}{1}$ unc. lat. ^{7} unc.

Obs. A beautiful species from the East Indies.

1179. NATICA FLUCTUATA.

N. testâ subglobosâ, pallidâ, lineis albis longitudinalibus flexuosis angulatim pictâ; spirâ brevissimâ,
acutâ; aperturâ magnâ, supernè acutâ, infra effusâ, rotundatâ; umbilico angusto, tecto; callo
columellari expanso, infra albo, crasso, supernè
castaneo, tenuiore: long. $1\frac{7}{10}$ unc. lat. $1\frac{5}{10}$ unc.

Obs. This is the finest specimen I have ever seen
of this extremely rare shell. Besides the longitudi_
nal white zigzag lines upon a fawn coloured ground,
there are four transverse bands, very little darker
than the ground colour itself. The dark chesnut
edging to the expanded columellar callus is a principal character of this shell.

1236. PYRAMIDELLA SOLIDA.

P. testâ conico-turritâ, lævi, albidâ, maculis fuscis,
oblongis conspersâ: anfractibus 9, breviusculis,
supernè depressione angustissimâ; umbilico par-
vo, rimâ circumdato: long. $1\frac{1}{10}$ unc. lat. $1\frac{3}{10}$ unc.

Obs. Besides the dark brown blotches, the shell
is mottled all over with brownish. From Tranquebar.

1401. TURBO BICARINATUS.

T. testâ subrhomboideâ, albâ, epidermide lutescente
indutâ; anfractibus tribus, ultimo maximo, cari-
nis duabus validis, setosis, setis per fasciculos mi-
nimos aggregatis; umbilico parvo, subtecto, extus
carinato, carinâ setosâ; aperturâ subtrigonâ, magnâ, infra subcanaliferâ, labio columellari planulato,

columellæ basi angulatâ: long. $1\frac{4}{10}$ lat. $1\frac{4}{10}$ unc.

Obs. A very singular shell, which we have placed in Turbo, because it approaches nearer to it in general form than to any other genus with which we are acquainted. We do not as yet know any of its affinities, though we have some reason for thinking it may be related to Cancellaria. Having given two representations of the shell, we shall not here describe it. We are informed that it was brought from Newfoundland.

1402. TURBO TÆNIATUS.

T. testâ orbiculari-subconicâ, tenui, lævissimâ, imperforatâ, albidâ, transversim rufo-vittata; anfractibus quinque rotundatis, ultimo multò majore; aperturâ ferè orbiculari, intùs margaritaceâ; columellâ subincrassatâ, extùs depressiusculâ: long. $\frac{17}{10}$ unc. lat. 1 unc.

Obs. A shell which approaches very nearly in general form to Lamarck's Turbo diaphanus: it is of a cream colour, with eight or nine reddish bands: the sutures are indistinct, and it is a very thin shell. Its locality is unknown to us.

1418. PLANAXIS PLANICOSTATUS.

P. testâ oblongo-conicâ, profundè transversim sulcatâ, costis inter sulcos planulatis: colore fusconigricante, aperturâ pallidiore, columellâ albâ: long. $\frac{9}{10}$ unc. lat. $\frac{1}{2}$ unc.

Obs. From the Gallipagos Islands.

1439. TURRITELLA CINGULATA.

T. testâ albidâ vel pallidè castaneâ, anfractibus tricingulatis, cingulis castaneis, crenulatis. long. $2\frac{1}{10}$ lat. $\frac{11}{10}$ unc.

Obs. The three crenulated transverse ridges form the characteristic feature of this species.

1442. TURRITELLA CINGULIFERA.

T. testâ transversè striatâ, albidâ, suturâ profundè impressâ, fuscâ : long. $\frac{3}{10}$ unc. lat. $\frac{1}{10}$ unc.

Obs. From the East Indies: a very common species.

1449. TURRITELLA SPIRATA.

T. testâ turritâ, albidâ, apice obtuso, anfractibus transversè costellatis, longitudinaliter fusco-fasci-tis, supernè ad suturam depressione complanatâ conspicuâ; aperturâ subrotundâ, labio externo in-tegro, recto; interno incrassato, reflexo: long. 1$\frac{7}{10}$ unc. lat. $\frac{1}{2}$ unc.

Obs. From the Island St. Thomas. The point has probably been worn off, it has nevertheless been closed by the animal, so that it may be termed decol-lated. Two circumstances are remarkable in this shell, the broad flat depression of the upper part of the volutions, and the straight edge of the outer lip. Aware that it is generically distinguished by this lat-ter circumstance from Turritella, we would not have added it to this genus had there been any more con-venient place for it. Two other specimens are among the shells which I bought from G. Humphrey.

1503. PLEUROTOMA CRYPTORRHAPHE.

P. testâ turritâ, transversè striatâ umbilicatâ; an-fractibus infra medium unicarinatis, lineâ supernè infra suturam profundè impressâ; caudâ brevi: long. 2$\frac{1}{4}$ unc. lat. $\frac{1}{2}$ unc.

Obs. The keel appears to be placed in the mid-dle of each volution, because the impressed line be-neath the suture is much more conspicuous than the suture itself.

1533. TURBINELLA CHLOROSTOMA.

T. testâ ovali, albidâ longitudinaliter costatâ, transversè striatâ, apice acutiusculo; aperturæ margine denticulatâ, parte internâ luteâ, canalis basi
fusco maculatâ: long. ¾ lat. ½ unc.

Obs. Two specimens of this shell are in the collection, one of which is without spots, and the other
has a row of dark chesnut spots along the middle of
the last volution, and a few spots of the same colour
close to the suture: the row of spots in the middle
of the last volution is so arranged that one spot
comes between each longitudinal rib.

1535. TURBINELLA FUSUS.

T. testâ ovato-fusiformi, apice basique acuminatis,
striatis, anfractibus supernè obsolete nodulosis,
suturâ canaliculatâ, columellâ 5 seu 6 plicatâ;
long. 7 unc. lat. 3 unc.

Obs. Of this shell, which is nearly related to T.
Scolymus, there are two specimens, of which one
has lost its epidermis and has only five folds on the
columella; and the other, which has six folds, re-
tains its epidermis: this species has not the large
tubercles of the upper part of the whorls that cha-
racterize T. Scolymus.

1543. CANCELLARIA OBLONGA.

C. testâ oblongâ, apice acuminatâ, basi rotundatâ,
anfractibus 5, leviter ventricosis, concinnè decussatis: long. $1\frac{2}{10}$ lat. $\frac{6}{10}$ unc.

1544. CANCELLARIA NODULIFERA.

C. testâ ovato-ventricosâ, apice acuminatâ, anfractibus 6, carinato-noduliferis, ultimo transversim
costato-striatâ, costis noduliferis, seriè superiore

majore: labio externo crenulato; long. 2¼ unc.
1¼ unc.

Obs. This shell is of a pale yellowish brown colour, with a white band near the base of the last
volution.

1552. FASCIOLARIA PAPILLOSA.

F. testâ fusiformi, apice papilloso, anfractibus transversè striatis, medianè nodosis; aperturâ intus lævi, caudâ longâ; long. 3,⁷₀ lat. 1¹⁄₁₀ unc.

1553. FASCIOLARIA PRINCEPS.

F. testâ fusiformi, aurantiacâ, anfractibus 7 superioribus nodulosis, sulcatis, ultimo ventricoso, sulcis
validis, distantibus; aperturâ transversè et inter-
ruptè rufo-lineata: operculo bifariam sulcato, ra-
diato; long. 8 unc. lat. 3¼ unc.

Obs. This handsome and exceedingly scarce
shell is covered with a dark brown epidermis.

1614. PYRULA VENTRICOSA, Nobis.

Ficus tenuis, magna, cancellata, &c. Martini, iii. t. 66,
f. 733.

P. testâ ficiformi, tenui, supernè ventricosâ, tenuis-
simè cancellatâ; costis transversis, rotundatis,
distantibus; spirâ depressâ; colore albido, brun-
neo-nebuloso; costis pallidis, brunneo articulatim
maculatis; aperturâ intus violaceâ: long. 4¼ unc.
lat, 2¼ unc.

Obs. This fine shell appears to us to be very
distinct from Lamarck's P. reticulata, and to accord
extremely well with Martini's figure above cited. It
is one of those remarkable shells commonly known
in this country under the name of Figs, but we believe it to be an extremely rare species, as we have
never met with another specimen. Its locality is
unknown to us.

1615. PYRULA GRACILIS, Nobis.

P. testâ elongato ficiformi, tenui, albidâ, brunneo-
nebulosâ, striis, longitudinalibus exilissimis, transversis eminentioribus, planulatis; aperturâ intus
brunneâ, labio externo albido; long. 4$\frac{4}{10}$ unc. lat.
2$\frac{1}{10}$ unc.

Obs. A shell of more slender proportions than
the other Figs, and apparently very distinguishable
by the characters given above. There are several
specimens in this collection, but the locality has not
been preserved with any of them.

1629. PYRULA COARCTATA.

P. testâ pyriformi, transversè striatâ, albidâ, longitudinaliter strigis aurantiaco-brunneis ornatâ;
anfractu ultimo ventricoso, ad basim subitò coarc-
tato, in canalem longam decurrente, supernè no-
duloso-carinato; spirâ depressiusculâ, apice mammillari; aperturâ intus sulcatâ; columellâ obli-
quissimè uniplicatâ: long 3$\frac{7}{10}$ unc. lat. 1$\frac{15}{16}$ unc.

Obs. This elegant shell very nearly resembles
the Pyrula Spirillus, *Lam.* in general form, the fold
at the base of its columella is, however, much more
oblique, and its mammillary point much smaller; it
is, moreover, differently marked. A reverse specimen of the same species is numbered 1630.

1631. PYRULA BULBUS.

P. testâ subglobosâ, lævi, pallidâ, longitudinaliter
fusco-strigatâ, aperturâ oblongâ, amplâ; columellâ
incrassatâ, medianè emarginatâ, basi acutiusculâ;
caudâ recurvâ, bicarinatâ: spirâ brevissimâ, pro-
ductiusculâ; long. 1$\frac{15}{16}$ unc. lat. 1$\frac{7}{10}$ unc.

Obs. This specimen has the outer edge of the
inner lip of a fine violaceous colour. Locality unknown.

1634. STRUTHIOLARIA OBLITA.

Str. testâ subturritâ, anfractibus 2 vel 3 superioribus
noduloso-carinatis, inferioribus supernè subcarina-
tis, lævibus, quasi pallio incolæ reflexo oblitis;
labio externo acutiusculo; long. $1\frac{8}{10}$ lat. $\frac{12}{10}$ unc.

Obs. A remarkable species, inasmuch as the
outer lip is thin and rather sharp-edged, and the lower
volutions are smooth, as if they had been covered
over by the mantle of the animal, being turned back
when in motion, and depositing a thin coat of testaceous matter. A rare species, from New Zealand.

1641. RANELLA VERRUCOSA.

R. testâ acuminato-ovatâ, verrucosa, albâ, ultimo anfractu seriebus tribus verrucarum; maculâ fuscâ
in summitatem singularum: labio interno trans-
verse aurantiaco-lineato; long. $1\frac{4}{10}$ lat. $1\frac{2}{10}$ unc.

Obs. A very singular specimen, in shape resembling R. bufonia; its white warts with a dark brown
spot at the top of each form its principal character.

1645. RANELLA PULCHELLA.

R. testâ fusiformi, albâ, anfractibus 7, cancellato-
granulosis; suturis validis, varicibus latissimus,
radiatim striatis, alternis striarum apicibus rotun-
datis, caudâ longiusculâ; long. $\frac{7}{8}$ unc. lat. $\frac{4}{8}$ unc.

Obs. This very pretty little shell is ticketed in
Mr. G. Humphrey's hand-writing " *The Finned Frog,
from Japan?*" A figure, probably drawn from a specimen of the same species, is to be seen in Chemn. xi.
t. 193, f. 1860-1861, which, however, is referred to
by Dillwyn as a variety of Murex Gyrinus, and by
Chemnitz himself is called " *Varietas notabilis Mur.
Gyrini, Lin.*"

1703. MUREX MONODON.

M. testâ subfusiformi, tenui, anfractibus 6 seu 7, rotundato-ventricosis, transversim costato-striatis,
asperis, irregulariter subquadrifariam varicosis:
varicibus spinis longis, recurvis, dentatis armatis;
suturâ validâ; aperturâ subrotundâ, labio externo
infra medium dente valido instructo; caudâ longiusculâ, subrecurvâ.

Martini Conch. Cabin. iii. t. 105, f. 987, 980.

Obs. This shell, of which there are two specimens in the collection, appears to have been reckoned
among the varieties of Murex ramosus; we think,
however, that it is perfectly distinguished by a strong
tooth placed below the centre of the outer lip, which
is evident in all ages of the shell; a longitudinal tuberculated rib is observable between the varices of
the upper volutions.

1704. MUREX MONODON Var.

M. testâ crassiore, spinis varicum brevioribus, anfractibus omnibus interstitiis tuberculiferis, suturâ
læviore.

1789. STROMBUS CRENATUS.

S. testâ subovatâ, ventricosâ, lævi, spirâ brevi, mucronatâ, anfractibus prope suturas elevatiusculis,
demum latè depressis, parte inferiore et ventrico-
siore profundè transversim sulcatâ; aperturâ amplâ, labio externo expanso, margine plicato, crenato; long. 7½ unc. lat. 5½ unc.

Obs. Three specimens of this fine shell, in various stages of growth, adorn this collection; they
are of a light chesnut colour, mottled with white,
and are all covered with a strong slightly foliaceous
epidermis. The largest specimen does not appear
to be full grown, for it has not thickened its outer
lip, which is white within.

1791. STROMBUS RUGOSUS.

S. testâ oblongâ, longitudinaliter plicatâ, transversè
striatâ, apice acuminatâ, anfractibus supernè nodulosis; ultimo anfractu alterâ tuberculorum mini-
morum serie instructo; aperturâ oblongâ, labio
externo intus striato, columellari valido, supernè
infraque transversim striato; suturâ crenulatâ:
long. 1$\frac{5}{10}$ lat. $\frac{5}{10}$ unc.

Obs. This shell approaches nearer to S. plicatus
than to any other species; from that it is, however,
distinguished by the second row of tubercles on the
last volution, by its longer spire, and by its rugosity.
The specimens are of a rusty brown colour, a little
mottled with white. From the East Indies.

1792. STROMBUS GRACILIOR.

S. testâ ovato-oblongâ, apice acuminato-pyramidali,
ad basim transversè striatâ, pallidè aurantiacâ;
anfractibus supernè nodulosis; labio interno tenui, expanso, externo dilatato, intus transversè
leviter sulcato: long. 2$\frac{5}{10}$ unc. lat. 1$\frac{4}{10}$ unc.

Obs. A general resemblance is observable between this and Str. Pugilis, from which it is principally distinguished by its smaller size, its acutely py-
ramidal spire, and its more slender shape. It may
possibly prove to be only a variety of that species.

1823. CASSIS CORONULATA.

C. testâ ovato-turgidâ, apice acuminatâ, lævi, albidâ,
pallidò rufo-subtessellatâ; anfractibus supernè serie unicâ tuberculis subacutis coronulata, superioribus cancellatis; varicibus duobus ad quatuor
rufo-maculatis; aperturâ elongatâ, labii columellaris margine inferiore simplice; columellâ basi
sulcatâ: labio externo intus denticulato, dentibus
obsoletis duobus vel tribus ad basim marginis.

Obs. This bears a great general resemblance to Cassis glauca, Lam. and might easily be mistaken for that species : the following are the particular characters by which it may be distinguished : a more elongated general form, its light brown markings upon a lightish ground colour, and its wanting the sharp teeth at the basal margin of the outer lip, as well as a projecting appendage at the corresponding base of the inner lip.

1824. CASSIS RINGENS, Swainson.

Obs. This shell cannot properly be arranged with the *Cassides:* in our opinion it forms a good genus, to which also *Dolium Pomum* should be referred. In the present Catalogue we have transferred the latter to the genus Cassis, in order that the two species might be brought close to each other. In this respect we have followed Swainson, notwithstanding our own conviction that they approach nearer in natural affinity to Dolium.

1826. CASSIS COARCTATA.

C. testâ cylindraceo-oblonga, læviuscula, albidâ, castaneo-variegatâ et interrupte fasciatâ, spirâ brevi, subacuminatà; dorso seriebus quatuor tuberculorum subobsoletorum ; aperturâ elongatâ, supernè coarctatâ; labio externo margine acutiusculo, intus dentato ; columellâ plicatâ; long. $2\frac{4}{10}$ lat. $1\frac{4}{10}$ unc.

Obs. Certainly not a common species, though we have met with it several times. We believe it to be a New Zealand shell.

1958. BUCCINUM MELANOSTOMA.

B. testâ ovato-oblongâ, aurantiaco-ferrugineâ, transversè sulcatâ et striatâ, longitudinaliter undatâ,

anfractibus convexis, suturâ validâ, aperturâ ovatâ,
labio interno fusco-nigricante, externo intus sulcato, albo, margine denticulato, aurantiaco, dente
quinto ab basim prominente.

Obs. Six specimens in the collection all accord
perfectly in the characters above given: the longitudinal undulations, or folds, are very prominent,
and the transverse ribs, or grooves, run over them.
It is remarkable that the fifth tooth from the base of
the outer lip is the largest, and that it corresponds
to a groove that is more deeply marked on the outside than the others. This shell resembles B. Tranquebaricum in general form; in the latter remarkable character, however, it will be found to differ
materially. There are some fuscous spots sprinkled
over the ribs.

1963. EBURNA PAPILLARIS.

E. testâ oblongo-conoideâ, politâ, albâ, punctulis nu-
merosissimis fuscis; spiræ apice papilloso; anfractibus rotundatis, supernè depressis; columellæ
basi acutâ: long. $1\frac{7}{10}$ lat. 1 unc.

Obs. One specimen of this pretty shell adorns
this collection, it is the second that has come under
our observation, another, which was in the African
Museum, being in Mr. Broderip's possession. The
species has not the spiral channel within, that dis-
tinguishes others of the genus.

1694. EBURNA AMBULACRUM.

E. testâ ovali, apice acuminatâ, lævi, albidâ, maculis
transversè oblongis, fulvis: spirâ brevi, anfractibus ventricosis, supernè canaliculatis, umbilico valido; intus lævi: long. $1\frac{4}{10}$ lat. 1 unc.

Obs. This shell approaches very nearly to E. spirata, from which, however, it may be distinguished

by the more ventricose volutions and the regularity
and smoothness of the inside of the umbilicus. We
are informed by Mrs. Mawe that it has been received
from Java.

1983. TEREBRA LINEOLATA.

Chemn. iv. t. 155, f. 1463.

T. testâ oblongâ, turritâ, lævi, albâ, lineolis longitudinalibus, subundatis, flavidis pictâ; anfractibus 7
rotundatis, basi sulcatis, margine superiore sulco
valido prope suturam: long. $1\frac{2}{10}$ lat. $\frac{5}{10}$ unc.

Obs. The figure of Chemn. above quoted is referred to by Dillwyn as a representation of Buccinum
vittatum, which our shell resembles in general form;
the sutures, however, are not crenulated, and it has
only one groove, close to the upper edge of each volution. From Tranquebar.

1984. TEREBRA STRIGATA.

T. testâ turrito-subulatâ, pallidâ, strigis longitudinalibus, fuscis, irregulariter ornatâ, anfractibus
obliquè longitudinaliter subplicatis, lineâ impressâ
centrali divisis: long. $5\frac{1}{7}$ lat. $1\frac{1}{7}$ unc.

Obs. The colours of this shell resemble those of
the Zebra, for which reason it may be considered a
very handsome shell; and it is extremely rare, only
a few specimens having been brought from the
Panama.

1985. TEREBRA-FUSCO MACULATA.

T. testâ turrito-subulatâ, acutissimâ, pallidè fuscâ,
anfractibus non ventricosis, lineâ impressâ supernè
divisis, superioribus obliquè longitudinaliter sulcatis, inferioribus læviusculis, fusco-maculatis;
areâ inter suturam et lineam impressam sulcatâ,
fusco-maculatâ; long. 4 unc. lat. $\frac{13}{10}$ unc.

Obs. We have formerly received this shell from Senegal, wherefore we at first supposed it might be Lamarck's *T. Senegalensis;* upon examination, however, it does not accord with his description. Our shell is of a light brown colour, the upper part of the volutions above the impressed line are regularly spotted with dark brown; the spots on the lower part of the volutions are arranged in rows, the upper of which is contiguous to the impressed line. The grooves of the upper volutions are interrupted by the impressed line. In the larger specimens the grooves become obsolete on the lower volutions.

1986. TEREBRA PUNCTULATA.

T. testâ turrito-subulatâ, læviusculâ, pallidè auranti-aco-fulvâ, lineâ prope suturam impressâ; suturâ validâ, crenulatâ; anfractibus planulatis, mediane lineis punctatis, transversis, plerumque duplicatis impressis; long. $2\frac{8}{10}$ lat. $\frac{5}{10}$ unc.

Obs. This shell is of an uniform pale orange brown colour throughout. In one specimen there are two pairs of transverse dotted lines on each volution, and in the other there is a single dotted line between the two pairs.

1987. TEREBRA TRICOLOR.

T. testâ turrito-subulatâ, longitudinaliter obliquè striatâ, anfractibus planulatis, supernè pallidè luteis, infrà carneo-fuscis, lineis duabus impressis, alterâ prope suturam, alterâ carmesinâ, ad basim notatâ, ultimo lineâ tertiâ, impressâ, basali, rubrâ, labio columellari elevato; long. $2\frac{4}{10}$ lat. $\frac{4}{10}$ unc.

Obs. There are two specimens of this shell, from the Island of St. Thomas: the upper part of each volution, above the first impressed line, is of a pale yellowish colour, the remainder of each volution being of a dark brownish flesh colour, and the lower impressed line of a bright crimson; on the last volution is another impressed crimson line near the base.

1989. TEREBRA NUBECULATA.

T. testâ turrito-subulatâ, albo et aurantiaco-nebulosâ, anfractibus longitudinaliter sulcatis, sulcis confertis, interstitiis sulcorum crenulatis, lineâ prope suturam punctis impressis notatâ; basi aurantiacâ; long. $2\frac{4}{10}$ lat. $\frac{9}{10}$ unc.

1990. TEREBRA NEBULOSA.

T. testâ turrito-subulatâ, læviusculâ, transversè obsoletè striatâ, albo et aurantiaco-nebulosâ, anfractibus superioribus longitudinaliter sulcatis, lineâ impressâ prope suturam notatâ; basi aurantiacâ; long. $2\frac{7}{10}$ lat. $\frac{9}{10}$ unc.

Obs. The two species above described approach each other very nearly in general appearance: in the latter the longitudinal grooves are more distant from each other, they do not extend to the lower volutions, and the space between the impressed line and the suture is rounder.

2014. COLUMBELLA FASCIATA.

C. testâ oblongâ, lævi, apice obtusâ, basi transversè sulcatâ, anfractibus albido fulvoque variegatis, supernè albis, suturâ validâ, sulco subobsoleto prope suturam: columellâ lævi; long. $1\frac{1}{10}$ lat. $\frac{7}{10}$ unc.

Obs. This is the largest species of Columbella we have seen; on a ticket in Mr. Budgin's hand-writing it is called " The white banded and variegated large Olive nut, from the East Indies, V. fasciata."

2094. MITRA SUCCINCTA, Swainson.

M. testâ ovato-fusiformi, albâ fusco-variâ; costis transversis carinatis, interstitiis serie binâ punctis, spirâ gracili, breviore; labio crenato.

Shell ovate-fusiform, with transverse carinated striæ, the interstices with a double series of punctured dots, white varied with brown; spire slender, rather short, lip crenated.

Obs. The shape and habit of this shell is intermediate between M. *granatina*, Lam. and M. *texturata*, having the more slender form of the first, and the shorter spire of the second. The whole shell is crossed by elevated, well defined, and somewhat carinated striæ, or rather ribs, sufficiently apart to admit of two series of linear punctures, divided by an indented line, between each rib. The spire is slender, and shorter than the aperture; and the outer lip obtusely crenated. The ground colour of the shell is white, marked by broad and somewhat interrupted shades of brown, disposed longitudinally; pillar 5 plaited. In another specimen the brown shades assumed the appearance of bead-like dots on the ribs.

2095. MITRA SULCATA, Swainson.

M. testâ parvâ, subconiformi, transversim sulcatâ, albâ griseo-variâ; fauce fuscâ; labio crenato.

Shell small, subconical, transversely sulcated, white varied with grey, throat brown; lip crenated.

Obs. In shape nearly approaching to M. *carinata* (Sw. Ill. of Zool. pl. 2. ined.) but its shorter spire gives it something the appearance of a Conœlix. The whole shell is crossed by deeply sulcated striæ, or more properly grooves; the interstices being convex on the body whorl, but rather carinated on the shoulder and spire, which gives to these parts an angulated appearance; the base is contracted, and not in the least recurved; the aperture is longer than the spire, and is brown within; the outer lip crenated, and the pillar five-plaited. The ground colour of the shell is white, with four or five longitudinal grey waved stripes, and transverse dotted bands of pale yellow between the grooves. Length nearly one inch.

2096. MITRA LEUCOSTOMA, Swainson.

M. testâ ovatâ, lævi, epidermide olivaceâ, lineis fuscis, capillaribus, transversis cinctâ : aperturâ effusâ albâ.

Shell ovate, smooth, epidermis olive with transverse, brown, capillary lines; aperture effuse, white.

Obs. Size and shape of M. lugubris, Swains. Length $1\frac{2}{5}$. Shell entirely smooth, white, but entirely covered by a thin olive epidermis, which forms a paler band adjoining the upper margin of each whorl: numerous, slender, and well defined brown lines encircle both the body whorl and spire, these lines are slightly indented, and, in some parts, appear as if minutely punctured. The base is without grooves, the outer lip is smooth, and the aperture pure white; suture uneven; pillar four-plaited; spire and aperture of equal length.

2097. MITRA RUGOSA, Swainson.

M. testâ subfusiformi, perforatâ, turritâ, rugosâ, decussatim sulcatâ; anfractibus angulatis, anfractu basali medio contracto; basi subrecurvâ.

Shell subfusiform, perforated, turreted; rough with decussated grooves, whorls angulated, basal whorl contracted in the middle, base sub-recurved.

Obs. The shape of this curious species comes nearest to that of M. *costellaris*, but the spire is longer in proportion, and the basal part less contracted. The whole shell is rendered very rough by

numerous deep grooves, which are decussated at
nearly equal distances; the interstices resemble ex-
cavated hollows, and make the elevated parts granu-
lated; the volutions are obtusely angulated, and the
middle of the body whorl contracted. Throat striat-
ed; outer lip crenated, base slightly recurved, pillar
five-plaited. Colour pale, slightly clouded with
brown. Length $1\frac{4}{10}$.

2146. VOLUTA PULCHRA.

V. testâ oblongo-ovatâ, subfusiformi, lævi, nitidâ,
carneâ, albido-maculatâ, maculis spadiceis triseri-
atim irregulariter dispositis, ornatâ; anfractibus
supernè adpressis, tuberculis acutiusculis, subcom-
pressis, coronatis: aperturâ supernè acutâ, columellâ 4-plicatâ. Long. $2\frac{4}{10}$ lat. $1\frac{1}{10}$ unc.

Obs. In general form this very beautiful shell resembles some of the elongated varieties of *Voluta
Vespertilio,* the spire, however, is more acuminated,
and appears as if contracted just above the first volution. The specimen before us is of a delicate flesh
colour with snow white specks, and there are three
bands formed of irregular spots of a rich chesnut
colour. We have heard that another specimen of
this extremely rare shell exists in the collection of
Mr. Spurrett.

2149. VOLUTA FULGETRUM.

V. testâ oblongâ, lævi, spirâ acuminatâ, apice papil-
losâ, lævi; pallidè carneâ, spadiceo anguloso-stri-
gatâ, (quasi fulguratâ) anfractu ultimo ventricoso,
supernè subangulato; aperturâ oblongâ, supernè
acutâ, labio columellari tenui, expansissimo: columella triplicatâ: long. 6 lat. 3 unc.

Obs. In size and form this shell approaches
nearly to *Voluta magnifica,* it is, however, easily dis-

tinguished by its acuminated, papillose spire, by the obtuse angle on the upper part of the last volution, and by its markings, which consist of acutely angular broad streaks of a dark chesnut on a flesh coloured ground. The left lobe of the mantle of the animal must have been very large, since the columellar lip is extended so as to cover half of the lower volution. This is the only specimen we have seen.

2150. VOLUTA AULICA, Solander.

Obs. There can be no reason to doubt this being the identical specimen which was described by Dr. Solander from the Portland Collection. As any information relating to the history of so beautiful and rare a shell may be interesting to our readers, we copy Dr. Solander's description, which has been communicated to us by W. J. Broderip, Esq. from the MS. in the late Sir Joseph Banks's library, together with the notices relating to it from the Catalogue of the Portland Collection and that from the Catalogue of the Calonne Collection.

I. *From Dr. Solander's MS.*

Spira apice mammillari.

Aulica. Voluta emarginata, oblonga, inermis, albo luteoque nebulosa, spirà conicâ: anfractibus obliquè planis: mamillâ lævi; columella quadruplicata. Habitat in oceano I.

M. C. P.

II. *From the Catalogue of the Portland Collection.*

4021. A very fine specimen of Voluta Aulica, S. a beautiful red clouded species of the Wild Music kind, its country unknown, unique.

' III. *From the Catalogue of the Calonne Collection.* ;

273. Aulica—le Courtisan ou le Nuage rouge.—
Courtier or Red clouded.—Voluta aulica, Soland.
This beautiful shell is unique. Its country is unknown, but presumed to be from some newly dis-
covered Island in the South Seas. M. P. 4021.

2151*a*. MARGINELLA GOODALLI.

M. subovata, extremitatibus subacuminatis, flavido-
carnea, albido guttata; spirâ brevi; anfractu ultimo maximo, supernè rotundato-angulato, suturâ
inconspicuâ; aperturâ angustâ, columellâ quadru-
plicatâ, plicis validis; labii externi margine interno denticulato: long. $1\frac{1}{10}$ lat. $\frac{7}{10}$ unc.

Shell subovate, rather acuminated at each extremity,
of a yellowish buff colour, with round white spots:
spire short, last volution much the largest, with a
rounded angle at its upper part; suture incon-
spicuous; aperture rather narrow, flesh-coloured
within: four strong folds on the columella, of
which the base is one: outer lip much thickened
and reflected, its inner margin denticulated.

Obs. This is the only perfect specimen I have
ever seen of this elegant little shell; there is, however, a single incomplete specimen among Mr. G.
Humphrey's stores. I have the pleasure of naming
it in honour of my excellent Friend the Rev. Joseph
Goodall, D.D. Provost of Eton College, &c.

2260. CYPRÆA UMBILICATA.

C. testâ oblongo-ovatâ, basi acuminatâ, supernè sub-
rostratâ, umbilicatâ, dorso ventricoso, pallido,
fusco-maculato; ventre subrotundato, albido;
marginibus rotundatis, albidis, fusco maculatis;
aperturâ, dentibusque subdistantibus, pallidissimè
subfuscis; long. $3\frac{1}{10}$ unc. lat. $2\frac{1}{10}$ unc.

Obs. This singular Cowry, of which we have only seen two specimens, neither of them in good condition, appears not to have been noticed by any author; it is principally distinguished by a deeply umbilicated spire, the upper part of the aperture being produced and rather reflected, and by its acuminated base: in general form it resembles a pear, and its colour and markings are like those of some varieties of C. Tigris. We are not acquainted with its native country. The other specimen is in our own collection.

2261. CYPRÆA MELANOSTOMA, Leathes MS.

C. testâ ovali, turgidâ, subfuscâ, transversè obsoletissimè brunneo-fasciatâ, guttulis elevatiusculis, niveis conspersâ; ventre convexiusculo, extremitatibusque albidis, lateribus dorsalibus subincrassatis, utrâque extremitate subfoveolatis; dentibus labii externi mediocribus, interni minoribus; interstitiis fusco-violascentibus; long. $2\frac{1}{10}$ lat $1\frac{4}{10}$ unc.

Obs. This Cowry, which we understand to have been brought from the Red Sea, does not appear to be uncommon; we do not, however, find it described either by Dillwyn, Lamarck, or Gray. It has been mistaken for C. Vitellus, to which it approaches nearly in general appearance. It has, nevertheless, been long distinguished from that species, and may be known by its want of the arenaceous transverse lines so characteristic of C. Vitellus; the teeth on the inner lip are smaller than in that species, and their interstices are of a brownish violet colour: the teeth of the outer lip are larger than those of the inner; and the whole margin of the shell is whitish. In its incomplete state it is destitute of the pearly white specks on the back.

2288. ANCILLARIA APERTA.

A. testâ oblongâ, cylindraceo-ventricosâ, aurantiacâ;
spirâ brevissimâ obtusâ; suturâ rotundato-impres-
sâ; anfractu ultimo cingulo basali unico, sulco supra varicem instructo, varice albo, obliquè striato;
aperturâ amplissimâ, pallidâ, supernè obtusâ, labio
externo ad basim edentulo, lævi: long. 1$\frac{5}{10}$. lat. $\frac{15}{10}$
unc.

Obs. A beautiful species, and apparently very
distinct from all those described by Mr. Swainson in
the 36th Number of the Journal of Science, Litera-
ture and Arts. It differs from A. effusa, the only
one with which, on account of its large aperture, it
could be confounded, in the following particulars:
it is a much less slender shell, it is not banded with
white, it has not a deep groove above the varix of the
columella, it has only a single belt above the said
groove, nor has it any tooth at the base of the outer
lip.

2330. OLIVA SPLENDIDULA.

O. testâ cylindraceo-oblongâ, albidâ, fasciis duabus,
alterâ supra medium, alterâ basali, utrâque maculis trigonibus fuscis, confertis notatâ: interstitiis
fasciarum maculis trigonibus fusco-nigris consper-
sis: spirâ brevi, mucronatâ; cingulo basali fusco
maculato; aperturâ intus pallidè fulvâ; columellæ plicis regularibus, basi carneâ: long. 1$\frac{1}{10}$
lat. $\frac{1}{10}$ unc.

Obs. A very beautiful Olive, and apparently very
distinct; the pale ground colour is finely relieved
by the two dark brown bands composed of triangular fuscous spots and larger intermediate rich dark
brown blotches. We have never seen any other
specimens of this Olive than those contained in this
collection, nor are we acquainted with its locality.

2331. OLIVA PATULA.

Voluta patula, seu aperta, Sol. MS.

O. testâ oblongâ, depressiusculâ, subalatâ; griseo-
lutescente, maculis fulvis pallidis adspersâ, spirâ
brevi columellâque supernè callosis; callo incrassato, albo, lævi, columellâ albâ obliquè sulcatâ,
plicâ majusculâ ad basim internam; cingulo basali
griseo-lutescente, bipartito, pallidè fulvo maculato: aperturâ pallidâ, subfuscâ, patulâ, supernè
subrotundatâ: long 1½ lat. $\frac{8}{10}$ unc.

Obs. From the Brazils. This is certainly a very
remarkable species, which we do not find noticed by
any author: its depressed form, large expanded outer
lip and consequently wide aperture, together with
the depression at the base of the body volution above
the varix and the large acute-edged fold at the base
of the columella distinguish it at once from all
others. The external colour of the body whorl above
the double belt is greyish yellow, through which are
sometimes seen pale markings of a fuscous colour,
these are not, however, always observable. In one
specimen, which appears to have been treated with
acid or to have had its outer coat otherwise abraded,
these angular fuscous markings are much more distinct. This is certainly not a common species; there
are, however, several remarkably fine specimens of
it in the collection of Mr. G. Humphrey. Two varieties may be distinguished, one of which is much
broader than the other.

2332. OLIVA BIPLICATA.

O. testâ ovali, griseo-fulvescente, longitudinaliter
substriatâ, lævi; spirâ subacuminatâ, suturâ subfuscâ; columellâ lævi, supernè callosâ, ad basim
biplicatâ; aperturâ, columellæ basi, cinguloque
basali violaceo tinctis; long. 1 lat. $\frac{6}{10}$ unc.

R

Obs. A pretty little Olive, of a very regular oval form, from the west coast of North America; its smooth columella, callous at the upper part, and having two small folds at the base, is its principal characteristic mark.

2333. OLIVA COLUMELLARIS.

O. testâ oblongâ, depressâ, fuscâ, apice, basi, fasciisque duabus albidis; labio columellari albo, incrassato, calloso; callo supernè inter superiorem labii externi partem et spiram interposito; plicâ unicâ ad basim internam columellæ; aperturâ supernè acutâ, subtus effusâ, margine albido; operculo tenui, lanceolato, corneo. Long. $\frac{6}{10}$ lat. $\frac{3}{10}$ unc.

Obs. The singularly incrassated, callous upper part of the inner lip separating the spire from the upper part of the aperture, gives to this shell a very extraordinary appearance, and forms the characteristic feature of the species. The inside of the aperture is dark brown, with a single, nearly central yellowish band.

2467. CONUS CINGULATUS.

C. testâ subcylindraceo-oblongâ, ventricosiusculâ, albâ, pallidè roseo nubeculatâ; spirâ sulcatâ, anfractuum marginibus elevatis: anfractu ultimo supra infraque sulcato, medio cingulo planato; columellâ basi subumbilicatâ; long. 2 unc. lat. $1\frac{1}{10}$ unc.

Obs. This is a very delicate Cone, which we do not find described by Lamarck nor figured in the Encyclopædia; it approaches nearly in shape to Conus bullatus, it is white with delicate rose-coloured irregular markings; its spire, as well as the upper and lower extremities of the last volution, is deeply grooved.

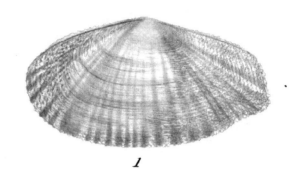

1

2

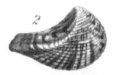

2

3

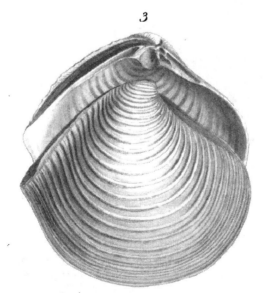

1 Tellina pulcherrima
2 Crassatella radiata (*Lyell*)
3 Mactra elegans

2

2

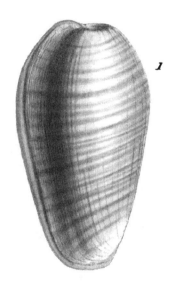

1

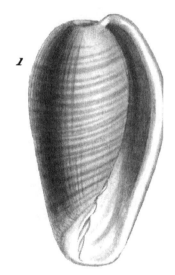

1

4

3

1. *Marginella bullata*.
2. .... *Goodalli*.
3. 4. .... *bifasciata*.

1

2

1. *Voluta Cymbiola*
2. ——— *pulchra*.

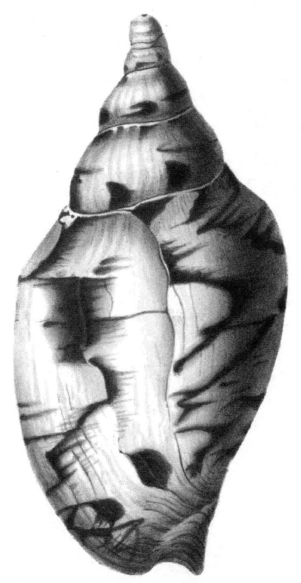

Scharf lithog.   Printed by C Hullmandel

Voluta Fulgetrum Sowerby in T C. 2149.

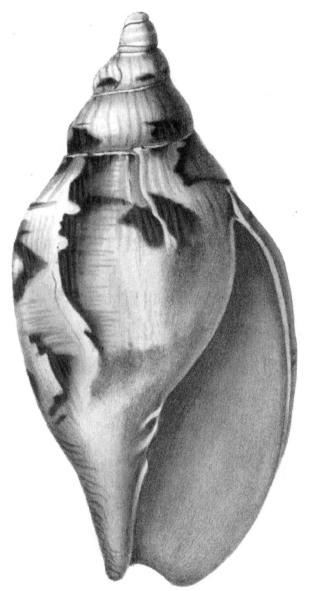

Voluta Fulgetrum Sowerby in T. C 2149.

Voluta Aulica.

LIBRAIR. DU PALAIS DES ARTS

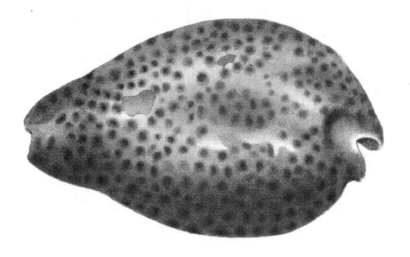

Cypræa umbilicata Sowerby in P.C. 22.v.

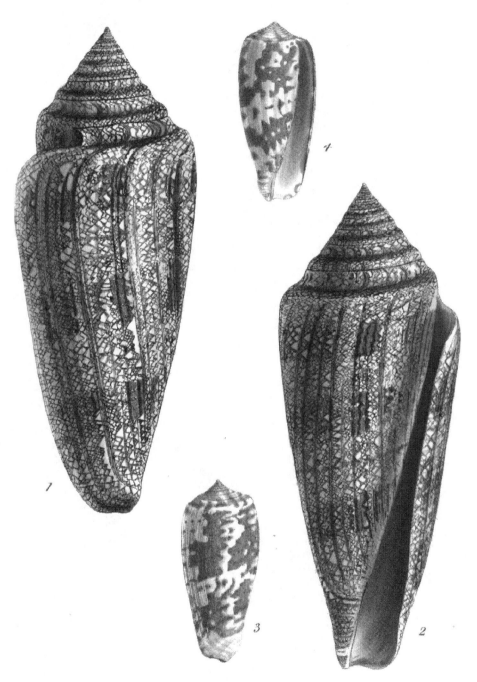

1. 2. Conus Gloria Maris.
3. 4. ..... vespertinus.

J. Fahey ad nat del.   Printed by C. Hullmandel

Turbo bicarinatus Sowerby in Tank: Cat: 1401.